GUANACASTE SNAPSHOTS

GUANACASTE SNAPSHOTS

AN ALBUM OF IMAGES AND MEMORIES OF
RURAL COSTA RICA 1965-1985

Second Edition

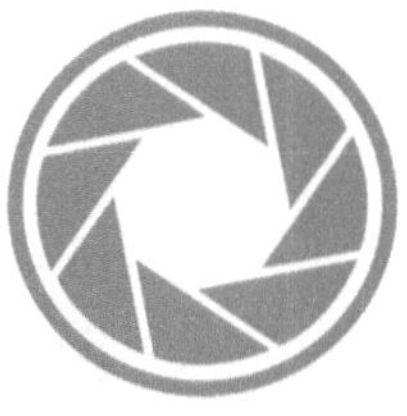

SUSAN GORDON

ISBN: 978-1-963068-70-2 (sc)
ISBN: 978-1-963068-77-1 (hc)

Library of Congress Control Number: 2024918136

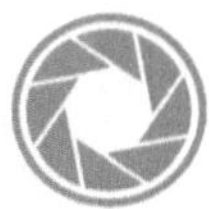

Contents

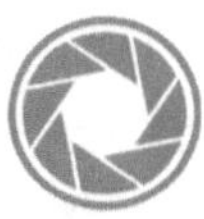

INTRODUCTION

I went to Costa Rica in 1965 when I was 22 and fell in love with a way of life completely different from anything I'd known until then. I met and lived with the people, places, and the language that forever changed my life and personality.

It's tempting to wonder who I might be today had I never experienced Guanacaste.

Who knew, at the time, that it would turn out to be the choice that determined the first half of my life's path?

For the first two years, 1965 and 1966, I was a Peace Corps volunteer. After that I made several short visits and then returned with Bill in 1973 for a "short trip" that turned out to be nearly ten years. During four of those years I taught at the local branch of the University of Costa Rica in Liberia, Guanacaste. The University required that I get an advanced degree to retain my position, so I left for 9 months to earn an M.A. at UCLA from 1979–1980. By the time I returned to Costa Rica to resume my teaching in 1980, I'd been bitten by the study bug and decided to leave Costa Rica the following year to continue at UCLA in the Folklore and Mythology Program where I completed a Ph. D. in 1986. In between, I returned to CR in 1983 for 4 months to complete my dissertation research. My last trip to Costa Rica was in 2007, with Michael, though I still maintain contact with good friends there. And now it's so much easier and fun with the internet and social media apps.

The vignettes in this collection, like a rotating ball of mirror chips are meant to provide varied, small glimpses of life and experiences of real people, my friends, neighbors, and at times, myself, over the nearly 30 years that Costa Rica was my second home. During the first two years, I probably romanticized and idealized it beyond proportion. By the end of my time there in 1983, I no longer viewed it so uncritically. I had become so acculturated that I didn't really question much of what seemed ordinary.

Some of the stories reflect personal experiences and involvement within the daily life of our community. Not simply observations *about* other people, these stories ARE stories because of my personal participation over time. This may disturb some readers. However, the reality is I was not simply sitting on the sidelines, taking notes or being a journalist, watching others from a distance; I was intimately involved with them. I never had any writing aspirations until I was working on my thesis; my professor said these descriptions had no place in academic or scholarly writing and suggested I separate them out. That suggestion led to my expanding the collection, keeping each story succinct enough to provide a "snapshot."

While there is no requisite order in which the stories should be read, I think they fall into two main sections. First, I try to give the reader an idea of the landscape and surroundings. Here you will find observations of nature, the river, the early morning, a cross-section of the townspeople and their ways of getting along with each other. Then I try to capture the essence of the lives of specific individuals as I interacted with them. In no way are they meant to paint caricatures or stereotypes. In addition, because of my interest in and study of folk traditions, narratives, and customs, some of the stories may include such details in their natural context, most notably the one about Don Goyo and the other about Dona Zoila.

I have used a lot of Spanish words and phrases throughout and therefore have provided a little glossary at the end of the book as a reference for those unfamiliar with Spanish.

All the experiences I relate actually happened in one way or another. I had the privilege of knowing people over a 30-year period, so I saw the many changes in their (and my) lives in relationship to and with each other. The stories are not "travelers' tales" or a journalist's feature about Costa Rica. They depict life in rural Costa Rica as it was in mid-20th century, before it became a trendy vacation spot. It is also part of my personal journey through that way of life.

In the last chapter I try to reflect on my own motivations (unarticulated and unconscious at the time) for going to Costa Rica in the first place. I have come to believe that when anyone leaves home for such an extended period, there must be some very deep and often unexamined reasons. I have tried to come to terms with why Costa Rica, during those years, became my "emotional home."

Visitors to Costa Rica today see a very different place from the one I knew. In fact, when I last visited in 2007, I felt like a stranger in many places. Today there are beautiful resort hotels, indoor plumbing, paved roads, internet cafes, and air conditioning. Television, telephones, and easy travel are taken for granted. These stories hopefully will provide little snapshots of a way of life that has nearly been eclipsed by modernity and fast-paced progress.

Of course, human nature doesn't change even as the external surroundings and the trappings of daily life do; so foreign travelers and visitors can still meet the kind of people I knew in Guanacaste with the complex range of human trials, intrigues, sorrows, and pleasures.

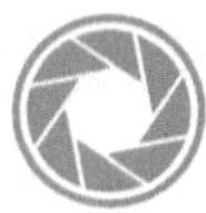

ACKNOWLEDGEMENTS

These stories come from a very deep place in my heart. The extent of my gratitude to all those friends and neighbors who mean so much to me is inexpressible.

To them, simply, *muchísimas gracias*, many thanks. I want to give special appreciation to my dear and trusted friend, Eny Maria Vargas. Many of the stories are deeply rooted in and extracted from our conversations and visits over the years. Now as this book is in revision, we are still in contact, with nearly 60 years of friendship.

The late Jim Kennedy gave me some very valuable and constructive suggestions when he read an early version of the manuscript. Robert Georges (RIP) was my mentor at UCLA who encouraged me to put these memories on paper in the first place, when he directed my dissertation work. Nina Karlin Jacob (MFT) helped me sort out and articulate many of the early family difficulties at the root of my emotional life. In 1992 Jay Kaplan, then director of the New York Humanities Council, invited me to submit for publication to his magazine *Culture Front* three of the stories, "Rio Tempisque," "Danielillo," and "The Gospel According to..."

I wish to give special mention in loving memory of Bill Shockley (1942-2013), without whom I probably would not have had many of these experiences and reflections. Bill passed away in a fatal, head-on motorcycle accident, several years after having been sober and healthy and living back in California. A sad irony. He was a good friend and a brother despite everything else.

I especially want to thank my wonderful partner, Michael Enav, who lovingly encouraged me with this revised project. My life changed direction for the better when I met him in 1995 and moved to Tel Aviv in 1998. I am more than grateful to him for all he has given me over these fulfilling years especially coming to terms with what I had accepted as "normal" really was not.

Please note:

The identity of all the individuals as well as the town have been changed. Some artistic liberties have been taken. I am solely responsible for any reflections or misrepresentations that may occur.

Perspectives

Elephants Balanced on a Spider Web

Un elefante se balanceaba
sobre la tela de una araña.
Y como esta no se rompía
fue a llamar a otro Elefante.*

One elephant balanced himself
on a spider web.
And since it didn't break,
he went to call another elephant.

By the late 1970s or early 1980s, hardly a Sunday travel section of large US newspapers missed advertising great deals for traveling to Costa Rica, the so-called "Switzerland of Central America." Packages included nature tours, fishing, white water rafting, Spanish language study, surfing, sea kayaking, wind surfing, and jungle visits to the cloud forest, all for the low special of $499, three nights, four days. Now lots of people considering a foreign vacation trip talk about going to Costa Rica. They even seem to know where it is! Which is different from when I returned to the U. S. in 1966 after my two years as a Peace Corps volunteer in that country. At gatherings of my parents' friends they would say in their all-knowing adult voice, "Oh, yes, Costa Rica, that island over there near Florida." Or when

I corrected them and said it is located in Central America, they would nod condescendingly and say, "Ah, of course, next to Missouri."

That Costa Rica was MY place off the tourist maps of the camera-toting, loud American tourists in plaid Bermuda shorts was fine with me. But in all the years of traveling and living there, I had never been a tourist, never visited the Cloud Forest (until 2007) or gone white water rafting, or deep-sea fishing. I never went kayaking or on a jungle trek, unless you count the one time I walked for two hours through the woods to a neighboring town to watch a soccer match with neighbors from the village I lived in. Admittedly, that was before any environmental organizations existed to "save the rain forest" and protect the virgin stands of natural hardwood trees. I had walked amid chopped and burned mahogany and rosewood stumps and wondered about the desolation but at the time never thought to question it.

Half a dozen years later in 1972 and back in the U. S., I had coincidentally met my old sixth grade boyfriend, Billy (now Bill), at a Tai Chi class in a church basement on 42nd St. and First Avenue in New York. A whirlwind romance convinced me to move to San Francisco to be with him, and inevitably came my need to share Costa Rica with him.

In mid-October, after the Watergate hearings and before President Richard Nixon's resignation, we set off on what was to be a six- month adventure to South America, with a stop-over in Guanacaste, Costa Rica, the place that held my soul as a second home, a place I had fiercely romanticized, the place that had changed my life and outlook forever. Conveniently, Bill had just won some money in a legal settlement for a motorcycle accident he'd had in New York City and was ready for an adventure; and I had nothing but three parttime jobs to give up. He bought and outfitted a 1966 long-wheel base, British-style steering Land Rover for the journey. He fashioned a raised wooden platform under which all our things could be stowed and on top of which we could roll out sleeping bags. I sewed little curtains and attached gold macramé ties embellished with Indian Sarna bells and other hippie-style tinkly ornaments.

We traveled to Mt. Lassen, Reno, Tonopah, and Las Vegas, Nevada, and stayed in Tucson, Arizona, with friends for ten days. We crossed the border at Nogales on Thanksgiving Day. My biggest concern was that Bill would be so earnest and honest with the sometimes infamous Mexican border crossing guards that he would show them the handguns he had insisted on taking along. They were stashed deep inside a trunk under the polished pine floor he had built. As it was, we had to empty the entire car but finally were able to get going when I gave the inspector a roll of dimes and one of pennies I had saved from Las Vegas. At the time Bill spoke no Spanish and seemed content to let me handle anything problematic in exchange for his driving and lighting the SVEA camp stove when we stopped to eat and camp.

Over the next three weeks, we traversed Mexico, overrun with young Americans seeking their personal Don Juan shaman and magic mushrooms; Guatemala, pre-civil war El Salvador, pre-Contra bivouacked Honduras, and post-earthquake but pre-Sandinista Nicaragua. Five days before Christmas, we crossed into Costa Rica. The changes were immediately observable. Suddenly even the ramshackle houses along the Inter-American highway were painted. Odd-lot Sherwin-Williams turquoises and dusty roses, those garish colors that don't sell too well in American towns, were all that was available in Costa Rican general stores. It's not that people necessarily preferred those colors. They just wanted paint. Take turquoise or take nothing. Other American brand items are sold that were notably inferior, too, reduced-size Brillo soap pads that gnarled up and rusted after one use, Palmolive soap bars that practically floated loosely inside the family-size wrappers, all "*elaborado en Guatemala*" or "*hecho en El Salvador*".

By the time we reached Costa Rica, Bill and I had been together a little over a year. Because I was afraid of "what people would say" if I told the truth, I told my old friends and neighbors in Tempira that we were married. They received him warmly. That warmth surprised him since he was unaccustomed to adults, especially older fatherly types, treating him like an appreciated son for merely being himself. His own father never did.

It only took nine months of Spanish lessons in the *cantinas* before Bill spoke fluently. By then he was as accepted a part of their world as I was. We were renting a little house, bought a few horses and some land to farm. Instead of the six-month adventure we had originally set off on, we wound up staying in Costa Rica for nearly nine years.

We began to run low of money around the same time that I was getting truly bored of having no responsibility outside of myself. That was when I got a job teaching English reading at the local branch of the university. By then Bill had developed a tri-partite career: He took on some specialty carpentry projects, making screen doors and paneled ceilings. He also tried to farm corn and rice on the plot of land he had purchased. His third, and perhaps main pastime was ingesting combinations of alcohol, over-the-counter cough syrups, depressants, or amphetamines, not to mention certain readily available (or easily grown) smokeable herbs known to lush climes. I continued to take care of anything problematic, until I was earning the living; he was responsible for fixing one meal a week, a baked tuna casserole for Friday night because I taught classes until late and didn't get home until around 9:00.

There **were** valuable things I gained from the relationship and, surprisingly to some, Bill and I continued to have a bond that lasted until his tragic death in a motorcycle accident in 2013, even though we divorced in 1983 shortly after our return to the United States. The Guanacastecos are especially incredulous about such staunch avowals. Once I visited about six months after Bill had taken his second wife on a honeymoon to Tempira. A former neighbor caught up with me walking down the street and reluctantly confessed that he had seen "Don Bill" with another woman and did I know about it? When I told him that not only did I know but that I wished them both well and hoped we could all be friends, I had given this neighbor more gossip material than he had bargained for! He could understand passionate hatred and bitter resentment or silent-suffering. He could accept feeling martyred love by one or the other. But just plain, dull, sibling-like kind regard? "Ah, you *norteamericanos* sure are weird!" he said as he shook his head in disbelief.

One of the greatest gifts I received from Bill was a new way of seeing nature. It is a gift for which I shall always be grateful. He taught me to look up at the stars on velvety dark nights; to watch columns of red ants shouldering slices of green leaves; to talk to baby parrots and puppies in their "language." I learned that little creatures live inside seashells, and that hummingbirds perch, that owls' wings flap silently, and that a scorpion will defeat a tarantula by clipping its legs if both are captured inside a jar. Two Costa Rican spider webs stand as a metaphor for the complex characteristics of many women's lives in Guanacaste. They are also part of the great gift of observation I received from Bill.

One spider web I would see just after dawn amid a dense, emerald-green crop of rice, across the road from our house. A wood fence enclosed the acres and acres of lush tall sprigs waiting to dry out in time for the November harvest. Between two of the rice shoots, hung the spider web. It looked bejeweled. The long rays of the sun sparkled off the silvery dewdrops pendulously bulging along the perfectly-spaced and symmetrical, silver spider threads. An aesthetically perfect creation produced by a tiny living being. The vertical strands formed an asterisk from the single vortex, with each concentric horizontal connecting thread straight and nearly taut. Only the very long outer "cross beams" dipped under the weight of the fattest droplets, which hung like a string of crystal chandelier bulbs, tiny rainbow charms on nature's knitted lace. A small spider sat curled in a ball in the center of her masterpiece, waiting patiently for someone else's misfortune to provide her breakfast. She was organized and technically highly skilled. She completed her task in a timely fashion and appeared to owe nothing to anyone.

The other spider web was reconstructed near our front porch every evening for a period of three weeks. By around 5:45 in the afternoon, at dusk, the spider, herself somewhat larger than a nickel coin but smaller than a quarter, would "rappel" onto the hibiscus bush and leap onto one of the vertical wooden house supports. She hung "guy wires" at random intervals and would begin to hoist herself from one wire to the next, forming the approximate circular shape of the web. She sloppily working her way round and round in concentrically smaller circles, just wanting to get the job done. By the time she'd tucked herself up in her seat in the middle of the web, one could detect many imperfections, places missed, zigzags that defied a pattern. It was a wonder the web was sound enough not to be torn from its anchors in the night breezes. But by early the next morning, the web was gone, totally disappeared, then again in the late afternoon, the spider reappeared and began this chore anew. Mesmerized, I watched her nearly every evening for a few weeks. It usually took her about forty-five minutes from beginning to end. I wondered when and why she took down her web. It was still there at ten o'clock but gone by four a.m. (I once got up to check!) That spider was unpredictable and not held by patterns of others' expectations. She was freewheeling and independent, not a perfectionist but always got a good-enough job done and cleaned up after herself. Then, one afternoon at the appointed time, she didn't show up. Had she died, living out a normal life cycle or had she merely found a more lucrative spot? These were questions I seriously pondered for a day or two.

It was around the same time that one of our small blue-green parrots (named Chito) learned the benefits of going into his cage around dusk. He was perched in the same hibiscus tree when an owl swooped threateningly close. The small parrot let out a squawk of utter terror and swiftly lowered himself to the tile porch floor and raced into his cage, pulling the door shut behind him with his little beak, before the owl had a chance to circle for a second attempt on his life. When I neared his cage, a trembling Chito, his iridescent blue feathers heaving with his hard breaths, was huddled beneath the little curtain sewn around his sleeping corner perch. He knew it had been a close call, I am convinced. I am still horrified when I think about that little bird's end, which was my fault. I had gotten into the car after an especially angry interchange with Bill and backed up without checking to see where Chito was. He was too close to the tire for the car completely to miss him. When I realized what happened I got out and scooped up the injured bird. He died in my hands. It was another high price for marital discord between two people who shouldn't have been married to each other. That little bird had an unusual spirit. His best friend was our dog Bouncer.

They would sit beside each other for hours, beak to shout, the dog sprawled, the bird balanced on one leg, the other tucked. If the dog decided to go outside, the bird, looking like a mechanical wind-up toy, would scurry after the dog, often just barely making it through the screen door to the back yard before it slammed shut. They were inseparable. Bouncer died or disappeared a year before Chito. He had been with Bill at the *finca*, and still we don't know if he wandered off and someone picked him up or if he fell prey to an alligator patrolling the river's edge. For all its benign appearances, the Tempisque River is known to have dangerous pockets of swift currents and dangerous reptiles. In some ways that applies to other aspects of life in Costa Rica, as well. In retrospect, however, my life in Costa Rica feels more like having been precariously balanced on the delicate yet steel-strong threads of a spider web.

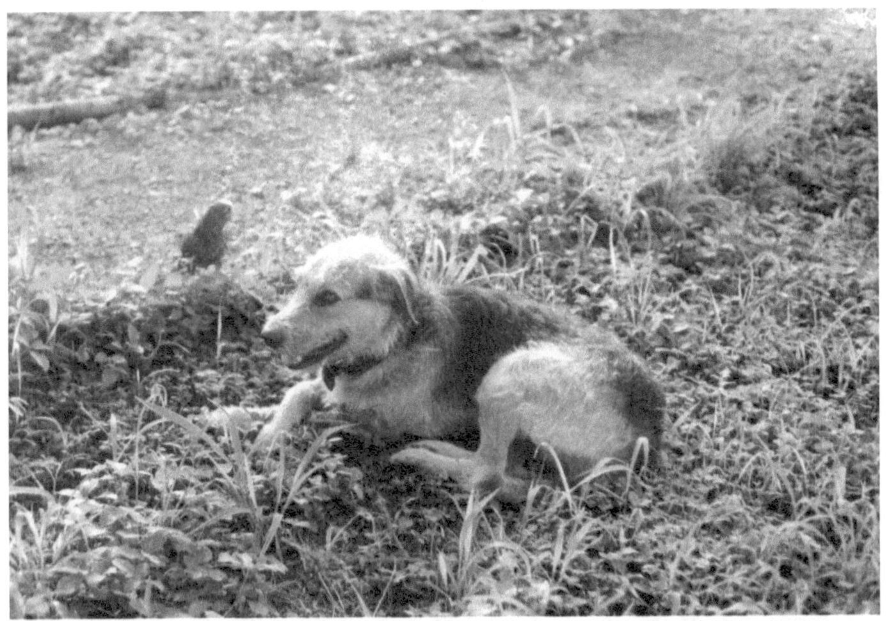

The country that comes into focus in my mind is not one that travel agents can arrange for tourists to visit. On the other hand, your four days and three nights will buy you a vacation that I am incapable of experiencing. Long-term residence, unlike a short vacation, produces memories that are fragmentary, selective, and like this book, episodic.

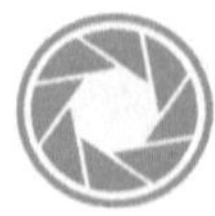

Depth of Field

Roads, Mail, and Phones

Before moving to Tempira in the second year of my Peace Corps service, I spent the first year in a small hamlet in the *frontera norte* (northern border region). In Canalete, the owner of the local cantina ran a generator and people could pay him to have electricity for their light bulb for a few hours in the evening, maybe. Sometimes, on rainy nights, there were no customers, so he'd turn off the generator early. Or sometimes he didn't have enough kerosene to run it and wouldn't turn it on at all. We received mail only once a week or whenever the "postman" went by horse for two hours through the mud and woods to Upala to bring the mail back in his woven jute *alforjas* (saddle bags). Sometimes the rain and mud prevented him from making the trip. It was not unusual for the mud to be so deep that the horse waded belly deep for the distance of several miles. The telegraph office was in Upala, too, so to communicate with anyone in San Jose or another city, one had to either send the message and money to pay for it with the mailman on the day he was going, or, if it was urgent, make the trip oneself. I tried hard to be very brave traveling thorugh the dense tropical brush, but my stomach was always in nervous knots, especially after the time I nearly met eye to eye with a green snake hanging from a tree branch that I was passing under. If one of the children accompanying me hadn't shouted for me to bend down, the snake and I would have collided.

Because it rains in the *frontera norte* nine or ten months of the year, vehicles back then could only enter during the driest time, usually around *Semana Santa* (Holy Week). That is when the bean wholesalers' representatives would navigate their huge canvas-covered rigs through the deep ruts of dried mud and drive into town to buy the harvest at the lowest possible price from the local farmers. The presence of those "city" men often motivated the young women to linger at the *pulperia* (general store) buying sugar or kerosene. Would anyone notice that they'd combed their hair with a little more flair and were wearing something a little more special than the usual errand-going house-chore clothes? Most of the buyers were from Palmares or other highland towns near San Jose. If the farmers found the price they offered was less than the price they could get from smugglers heading north, they hurried to see if they could still get in on a contraband deal before the city buyers left the area. If they missed out on both, they would be stuck with their entire harvest without any buyers, legal or illegal.

Nobody in the government seemed to pay much attention to the commercial arrangements or the inadequate transportation and communication facilities in this remote region. People referred to the area and to themselves as "*abandonado*." But every four years, presidential candidates made quick visits to the area hoping to find some eligible voters. Much of the population consisted of Nicaraguans who never bothered to become Costa Rican citizens. They had little or no schooling, no rights, and little money. With a very fluid, unpoliced border, they could come and go as desire or necessity dictated. A little problem with the law or an angry creditor might call for a quick trip across the San Juan river to Nicaragua, or vice versa. Most of the residents in this region weren't registered citizens, they had no voting rights. As a result, they had a hard time getting the attention of legislators or ministry officials who could help them with some basic community infrastructure, such as concrete drainage pipes needed to build an all-weather road, health services, latrines, or pumps for wells to provide an alternative to drinking river water which carried parasites. Every so often small community delegations went to San Jose to visit transportation ministry officials only to wait for hours in the minister's ante-room and then be granted a five-minute audience with some officious sub-functionary. He would tell them how "sympathetic the *Senor Ministro* was to their situation, but *lo siento* (sorry!), the road building equipment they requested was busy in another part of the country" (perhaps near the president's farm or another high priority spot!). "Of course," he would tell them, "contractors' solicitations and bids were being accepted right now for their very project, but no promises could be made at this time." The delegation never really knew just how low they were on the list of political priorities, but everyone developed a marked cynical streak about governmental intentions to help their area. They knew that politicians were out wooing and winning voters in other sections of the country. They knew, too, that there was a close correlation between every president's home region and new development projects that would be undertaken during his term of office. *Asi es.* (That's just how it is.) There was no representation in the National Assembly from this area which was actually represented by the town of Grecia, near San Jose. So with few registered voters, no local representation, no "interested" politician, no clout, they had little hope of achieving any road or other connection to the rest of the country. People would continue to depend on their horses and ox-carts until something would happen.

There was a small plane service from Cañas, a city in Guanacaste, along the Interamerican Hightway, on the western side of the *cordillera* (the volcanic chain of mountains running through all of Central America). It was supposed to come twice a week, but you could never count on it or on the conditions that would allow the plane to land. If the pass over the *cordillera* was socked in with clouds, the plane wouldn't attempt the trip. If it did manage to get through, but some lone cow was meandering on the dirt and gravel runway, the plane couldn't land. The pilot would circle once, giving someone time to chase the cow away, but if no one was there, he would just fly back without landing at all. I used to worry a lot about how I would get out of there if I had an appendicitis attack. I had heard about others who simply died because they couldn't get to a doctor, like Doña Pancha's little six-year-old who had such a severe case of round worms that they were in his lungs, and when they crawled out of his nose, he choked to death; or the woman who bled to death after a breech delivery of her baby. God's will is invoked with near-mantra repetition: *"si Dios quiere"* (if God wishes), or *es la voluntad de Dios* (it's the will of God), as an explanation for everything that cannot be questioned or acted upon in any human way. Trying to organize community folks to even attempt to push for change would be considered going against *la voluntad de Dios.*

Because of the various communication and transportation obstacles, and because there was so little progress to report in my Peace Corps job, it was easy to avoid contacting the world beyond this small village. I simply didn't bother after a while. I was, after all, a Peace Corps volunteer there to do a job of "community development," but there were no reporting procedures, no site visits from the San Jose staff, no support from anywhere. So I just got along doing with what I had, perfecting my language skills, to be sure, since no one spoke a word of English beyond the habitual "goo-by my lof" from 13 year old boys trying out their budding machismo. The reason I was sent to this place in the first place was to replace the previous volunteer who had actually been "banished" from the southern region instead of being sent home. Her "crime"? Helping another volunteer elope with an Italian Count. (Don't forget we're talking about 1965!). So the townspeople never quite understood why the sudden appearance of a young, single American girl in their midst. Her name was also Susan, but in most ways we were total opposites—she was short, cute, fluent in Spanish and flirtatious; me tall, plain, just learning Spanish, and very shy. But being Susan and American and this odd thing called a "*miembro del Cuerpo de Paz*" (Peace Corps Volunteer), allowed the people of Canalete to presume other non-existent similarities. Once she left, I was on my own but still called *La Otra Susana*.

After four months of not hearing from me, the Peace Corps sent two staff members from office in San Jose to look for me. They flew up for a "site visit," the first time anyone from the office had seen the conditions of that little community with two *pulperias,* a two-room school house, and four or five houses in the center. Then and there, they offered to transfer me to a more accessible area, to a town where a committee had actually requested a volunteer to work with them on community projects. So I moved to Guanacaste.

That town was Tempira which seemed refreshingly modern in contrast to Canalete. It had a bus that lumbered through town four times a day, electric lights every night until 9:00 p.m. or even later if there was a dance at the cantina, movies every week or two, and a telegraph and post office right in the middle of town. Being able to send telegrams to my Peace Corps pals in other towns was a new found luxury. I could wire to say when I would visit or to request a book or other item that they could merely hand to a bus driver who was coming this way.

Making a phone call was another matter. The closest phone facility was in Liberia, the provincial capital about 35 kilometers away, along a road that was only about two-thirds paved. The rest, the part nearest Tempira, was like a heavily rutted washboard and periodically scraped by a backhoe sent from the Ministry of Transportation and re-graveled with large stones. After a few days, though, the stones would once again be pushed aside by the passing trucks and cars treading the same path and the ruts were back. A ride along that bumpy portion of the road was a total body experience: starting with one's butt, which bumped so hard you could feel your insides slamming against your ribs. I often had to to clench my teeth just to keep from biting my tongue on a downward bounce! Sometimes I took an offer for a *paseo*! Riding four girls in the front seat and five in the back of Ana's brother Eddy's 1957 DeSoto with worn-out shock absorbers was a riot of giggles and singing, and certainly faster and more fun than traveling in the old blue converted school bus (named *El Consentido*, the spoiled one) that served as public transportation.. But in any vehicle, it was always a relief (especially to the bladder!) to reach the paved part of the road (right near the turn-off to a big *Liberacion Nacional* party leader's farm) for the remainder of the ride to Liberia.

The phone was located in the old office of ICE, *Instituto Costarricense de Electricidad*, the national utilities company. There was one phone for calling the international operator in San Jose, and a few phones to reach domestic operators, also in San Jose. People waited their turn for the attendant to help them. I would write down the number to be called and the attendant would place the call. Then he would tell you which little booth to go in once your party had been contacted. The attendant kept track of the length of the call and charged accordingly once you hung up. Only occasionally did I place such calls to the United States to talk to my parents. Usually it was easier, if not faster, to write them letters and send them slides with explanations of each picture. That was how it was in 1965 and 1966.

By 1973, most houses in Tempira had electricity and running water. Nicomedes, the young assistant, was about to take over as *telegrafista* from Don Ignacio, Nacho for short, who was about to retire. Nacho was famous for having a big mouth. If anyone got a postcard or telegram, he was the first to know its contents. He was the well-known source of much newsworthy gossip. Unless a postcard was enclosed in an envelope, Nacho would read and quicky and authoritatively disseminate the message. People in Tempira were more relieved than saddened by his decision to retire.

When he left, other things changed, too. The old wooden building which housed the post office on one side and the jail cell on the other, was replaced by a cement block structure. The old building, like many of the traditionally built houses and stores, was set up on large boulders. Now there was a poured concrete slab foundation and a solid wall separating the jail and the post office. Im the old building there was just a thick wood lattice-work door with a large chain and padlock. A little patience and an emery board would have been sufficient to saw through the rotting wood and provide escape to any enterprising culprit. The cell itself was equipped with a cot and a chamber pot. Detainees were usually held overnight because of some disorderly behavior or involvement in a machete fight. Anything more serious required taking the prisoner to Liberia for booking and jailing in the *cuartel*, the provincial jail.

When the new post office/jail structure was whitewashed with lime and the wood service counter was set up, the place was officially opened for business. Nico had his telegraph equipment set up behind the counter, and now a phone booth stood near the door. The phone line had finally reached Tempira! Nicomedes was in charge of the phone, too, with procedures similar to those practiced earlier in Liberia. But when he calculated the charges and someone didn't have enough money to pay for the call, Nicomedes would write down their name and the amount owed in an old school notebook with hand-drawn columns . He sincerely believed when people said they'd pay him tomorrow. Often five or six people might be waiting to make a call. They would stand around and chat, always a bit distracted, straining to overhear the phone conversation in progress. Everyone in turn tried to secure the door to have a private conversation, but it was made of flimsy wood and glass, so those outside could always catch snippets. Nicomedes, however, was so discreet that even when he was the only person who could overhear conversations, or was the only one who knew to whom calls were directed or from whom they were received, he never shared that information with anyone. Even if someone asked, he would just smile, look embarassed, and change the subject.

Then one day the phone booth suddenly disappeared. Completely. Dirt marked the square in the corner where it had been. It seems that the ICE (the telephone company) decided to move the public telephone to the home of the retired Don Nacho. Apparently Nicomedes had been too trusting and willing to let people make calls on credit. Empty promises to pay filled his wrinkled notebook. ICE had issued him a warning, and he tried to collect the money, but finally when he owed nearly 8000 colones (about $1000 at that time), they moved the service out of the post office. It seemed strange to me that people didn't come up with the money since they were so uneasy about making or receiving calls at Nacho's house. But the phone was moved despite his recognized proclivity for exaggeration and lies. His house was at the far end of town, dark, and out of the way on rainy nights. Phoning became only a tool for the most necessary and business-like calls. Hanging around the phone/post office/jail to socialize and eavesdrop abruptly ended.

On a brief visit in 1989, I noticed a few changes. Aside from seeing everyone noticeably older, fatter, and grayer in the normal course of aging most everyone was the nearly the same. I found the once-dusty streets of Tempira now paved with thick, black macadam. I learned that some people I knew, or their children or in-laws, had been killed by speeding cars or trucks as they walked or rode horses along the highway. Others had died in motorcycle accidents while driving drunk.

During my visit, coincidentally, a real highway from Cañas to Upala (the region where I had first lived) was being inaugurated. Now, instead of three days in an ox-cart, the trip can be made in less than forty minutes. Because of the Nicaraguan Revolution in 1979 and the political interests of the US in the region in the 1980s, the northern frontier region became a high, strategic priority, if not for the Costa Ricans, at least for the United States and President Reagan's policies.

I went to look for Nicomedes in his post office. I found him out back macheting the ever-encroaching greenery. He went through the back door and met me inside. I noticed that his old telegraph equipment was gone, in its place an oblong box. "*Idiay*? Nicomedes, what's this? no telegraph service?"

"Nope, now it's all radio-ed out these days."

I asked him what happens if the electricity fails. He laughed and said, "Well, there's no service until the electricity's restored." Then thinking for a few seconds, he said, "Makes you wonder if it wasn't better the old way, huh?"

Now lots of families have telephones in their own houses. The public phone was moved out of Don Nacho's to another spot and was still utilized by some who didn't have home phones yet. The biggest complaint I heard about the private home phone service had to do with secrecy.

"Before," they said, "you could see who was going where, when they arrived, when they left, and there was some idea, at least about who was responsible for spreading, or inventing, certain stories. Now anyone can sit on the phone in their own house, behind shutters, screens, or curtains and invent and relay information without being seen. Now you don't know exactly whom to distrust."

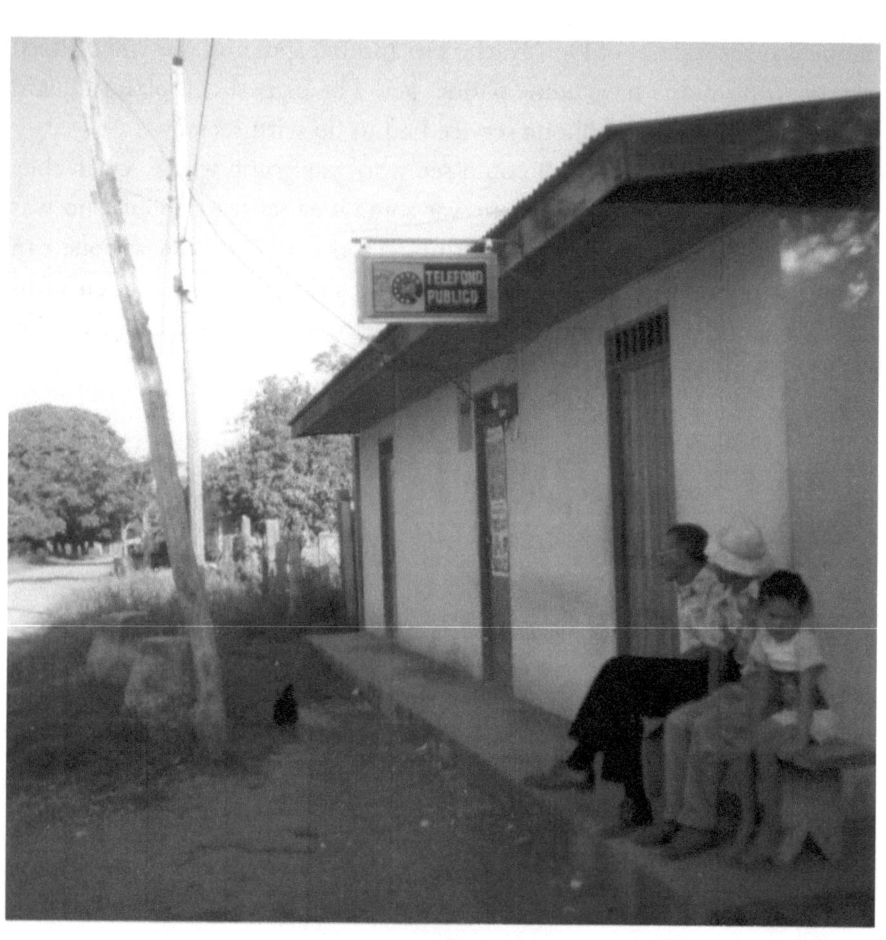
TELEFONO
PUBLICO

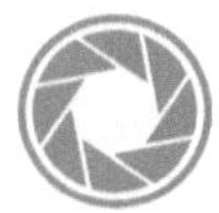

In Focus

Local Talents

In Tempira, as in many small Costa Rican towns, most everyone is related by blood or by marriage. They greet each other "*q'hubo prima*? (Hey, cuz, what's going on). People know each other by what they DO best. That's just how it is in this town of eight hundred *cristianos*, as they say. Here are some examples among the neighbors of the local talents that characterize each of them.

Don Alberto Fulano, was one of the oldest brothers of the large and prosperous family in Tempira. He was highly regarded for his vast knowledge about horses: which ones were trainable for prancing and high-step dancing in festival parades, and which would be better at herding cattle. Just by observing a horse's behavior for a few minutes, Don Alberto could tell what was wrong or right with the animal. Whenever a horse was bitten by a tarantula spider, Don Alberto was unafraid to lift a stallion's hind leg to inspect its ankle. The horse seemed to sense from Don Alberto's calm confidence that he was in competent hands. Those big hairy spiders, often the size of a man's fist, live in holes they dig in the ground, frequently in pastures where horses graze, so it is not uncommon for grazing or sleeping horses to be bitten. While not fatal, a tarantula bite causes the horse's hoof, like a big toe nail, to fall off. As a precaution against the spiders, cowboys usually rubbed a tar-like mixture *(alquitran)* on the horses' legs, giving them a look of wearing black socks or boots. Don Alberto was also an expert in selecting well-fitting saddles, cruppers, and bits, judging which bit best fit the jaw size or where to adjust one in case it was rubbing sores inside a beast's mouth. He had favorite saddle makers in Liberia or Santa Cruz who knew that he expected high quality workmanship and would immediately recognize and reject anything shoddy.

Don Alberto continued to ride his *macho mula* (large horse crossed with a mule) sometimes bareback until well into his seventies even though his brother, a famous San Jose doctor ordered him not to. Even his family's pleas went unheeded, despite his having taken a bad fall that was to be the beginning of his end. But with a wink and a smile, he would quietly ignore them. In his formal dignified way, he would shake his head from side to side, saying that none of them could understand, that his life would be over if he had to give up the saddle. It wasn't too long afterward that he peacefully died at home. Shortly after his funeral, his daughters commissioned a large wooden cabinet with glass doors to be built. They set it in a corner of the living room. There they hung their father's horse-hair trimmed quilted leather *albarda* (hornless saddle with a long "skirt) and put all the other *aperos* (gear) along with his wide-brimmed canvas hat on hooks inside the display cabinet as a memorial to him. His daughters' devotion was well known, and they saw this cabinet as one more way to honor him and what he loved most. Today his nephew Carlos, straight-back gaucho hat reins held high in his hands can be seen rehearsing his own high-stepping parade horses in the late afternoon. Most people will tell you that Carlos is the town's horse authority now.

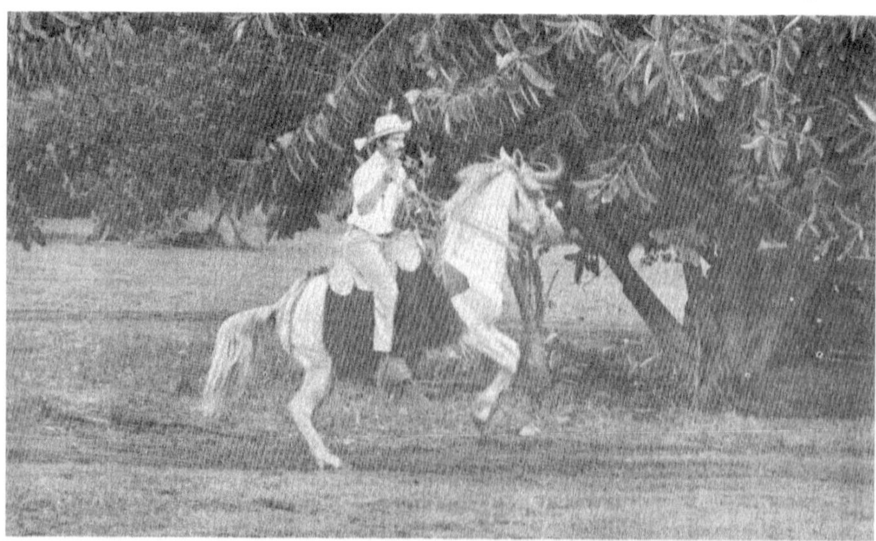

Doña Juanita (Nita, for short), Don Alberto's widow, used to be known as the best dressmaker in town. She used to keep a stash of the latest Lana Lobell catalogues, *Simplicity* magazines from the U.S., and issues of *Burda,* a fashion magazine from Germany so the girls and ladies could select their clothes from current styles and fads. These girls were much more fashion conscious than I or my plain Peace Corps pals were. There we were in our little Peter Pan collars and wrap-around skirts, while these girls here really knew how to dress in great colors and becoming styles and to use make-up with the skill of any big-city sophisticate. They could tell from the pictures just how an outfit would look. And if they didn't like every single feature in the picture, Doña Nita could mix and create what they wanted, sometimes choosing a collar from this dress, sleeves from that one, and the bodice from still another. Silky blouses and form fitting pants were popular while we Peace Corps girls had been told we had to wear skirts out of respect for the local culture! Instead, we just looked frumpy while they looked stylish. Soon I, too, was asking Doña Nita to make outfits for me so I could look "in" with the other girls.

Doña Nita never seemed hesitant about making that first snip in a new piece of cloth. She was bold yet careful with her sharpened scissors biting out the shapes, be it on a well-behaved gabardine for school uniforms or slippery sateens or sleazy nylon for party dresses. Using only each customer's taped measurements that she kept recorded in a notebook, she knew exactly where to stop cutting, turn a corner, or put a notch. No paper patterns for her! Her nub-like fingers held the cloth steady as her feet rocked back and forth on the old Singer treadle machine. She worked from morning until night on many days, especially before a big dance, the start of the school year, a wedding or other grand occasion when the demand for new outfits was highest. Working at night was difficult as there was only one overhead bare light bulb and lots of mosquitoes and moths buzzing around the light. But she always seemed unfazed as she calmly worked her magic on what only hours before had been a swath of fabric rolled in a plastic bag.

By the late 1970s, most girls and women were buying their clothes ready-made in Liberia or San Jose; and thanks to MTV, they could easily keep up with the "*moda*." Doña Nita no longer sews since Don Alberto and son, Aristides, died. She says it's because her eyesight is getting worse and laughs when she says she's lucky to find her way out of bed. Now she spends most of her days watching soaps and game shows on the porch from her favorite wooden rocker from Nicaragua. But she still has an eye for fashion and how things are made and thinks nothing of inspecting hems or side seams or admiring the design stamped on things I wear during a visit. She marvels at the clothing from the U.S., but than we talk about how nearly everything I have on actually was made someplace else, outside the U.S. She understands well what cheap labor can do. All those store-bought things the girls wear these days are much less expensive than what she would need to charge for her time to make the same item. Her dressmaking skills are no longer needed. She left a bereft family at the age of 105!

Don Pablo Sutano, a soft-spoken old-timer, had a condition that created whitish-pink patches on his otherwise coffee-and-cream color face and arms. As a young man, Don Pablo had worked for ten years loading banana boats in Panama. Ever since he returned to Tempira in the early 1960s talking "all that crazy talk" about workers' rights to strike for decent wages and benefits, he's been known as the town "communist." No one pays particular attention to him, not even the workers. The Revolution probably won't begin in Tempira any time soon. Slightly bent, but still stocky, Don Pablo usually sits leaning on his walking stick, on one of the wooden benches on his porch or near the park. He passes long hours chatting brother, Don Rómulo (nicknamed Don Pinche), who used to be the policeman when the conservative Opposition coalition was in power. That right-wing coalition is even more anti-communist than the more liberal *Liberacionistas*, but the two brothers avoid heated discussions although they sit together for hours, day after day, year after year. Their sister, Margarita, who never married, shares the house with Don Pablo and cooks, cleans, and washes his clothes as though she were his wife. Don Rómulo has a house and wife of his own.

Doña Solemne de Fulano, along with her daughter Dalia, too, is known for making the best "*tipico*" baked goodies, *tanelas, empanadas,* and *rosquillas*, containing corn and grated smoked cheese and sometimes a heavy dose of cinnamon. A few days before Christmas, she makes gallons of *chícheme,* a corn and cinnamon drink that is left to ferment for a few days and leaves a prickly sensation on the tongue of the imbiber. By the week after New Year's, the *chicheme* might even be strong enough to make you feel a little light-headed. Doña Solemne is also known for the ferns and other greens she cultivates in tin-can planters in her yard. She is happy to give away plants since she says that God owns the plants, not human beings. We only take care of His creations.

"Papito" used to be known as the town drunk. Once he even sold his little daughter's school uniform to get money for alcohol. He would drink anything, even cheap perfume or after-shave cologne would do if he were thirsty. While he often approached people in the street to ask for a few coins, no one really considered it "begging," merely asking for a "loan." It was not uncommon to see him, tortilla-dough pale and unshaven face, torn shirt and stained trousers, slumped up against the locked door of the cantina as the morning dawned. Sometimes these binges would go on for three weeks. No one is quite sure what happened to Papito. Maybe he found God, maybe found his way to an Alcoholics Anonymous meeting in San Jose, or maybe he just stopped "cold turkey." One day, though, everyone noticed that Papito no longer drank and was no longer the "*pobrecito*," object of pity that he had been. Of course, there are plenty of other young alcoholic extremists to take his place. Papito had retained his title for so long that that when he recovered, they knew him as the one who *used to be* the worst drunk in town.

Hirsonisis Trejos, a transplant from San Jose, was known as the proud owner of the local movie theater and the only diesel-powered generator providing electricity to the town before the rural electricity cooperative began functioning in the 1960s. The generator also powered the dance salon and *cantina* run by his wife, Magda. In addition, he was the owner-operator of Tempira's only taxicab. But despite his hard-working, entrepreneurial spirit and efforts, Hirsonisis was both pitied and disdained, for he was even better known as a "*cabron*." That is probably the worst thing a man can be called, since it means that his wife has another man but he, the husband, does nothing to restore his pride. (Presumably, doing something would include things like leaving her or committing some violent act, what they always refer to in the newspaper reports as a "crime of passion.").

Hirsonisis' wife, Magda Mengano, became an alcoholic herself after years of serving beer and sugarcane "*guaro*". She spent her days chatting, teasing, flirting, listening to the troubles of her cadre of regulars, and dispensing advice, as she refilled their empty glasses and kept her own glass filled under the counter. But it was not merely hard work and long hours that ensured Magda's success as a *cantinera*. She couldn't have kept the business going without the help of a rich benefactor. Every now and then, a shiny, white Land Rover jeep would pull up and out would step a paunchy, older gentleman rancher, an accomplished horseman from a ranch near the Nicaraguan border. Part of the benefactor's "investment returns" apparently included personal servicing by the talkative bar matron. For someone who let the world in on everyone else's secrets, she at least managed some discretion of her own. The distinguished-looking gentleman, Don Victor Manuel, was well-known for owning and "renting" some of the best seminal Brahma bulls in the province. He never missed an opportunity to parade his pure-bred, steel-gray Andalusian horses in local *fiestas* throughout the country. He was easily recognized by his handsome black padded leather saddle and stirrups studded with real silver, not imitations of stainless steel. Don Victor Manuel was elegant and donned only the most extravagant finery for his equestrian performances. The "*laka-laka*" (chit-chat) reported that this portly and powerful gentleman not only gave Hirsonisis's wife the money to set up the *cantina*, but also enough to buy the electrical generator, and most likely the movie theater and even the taxicab. It was too good a deal for Hirsonisis to turn down, even though he received much open and public scorn from his wife. Everyone could see how pathetic he was. In fact, it was embarrassing for onlookers to see her sharp humiliation and open mockery of him. She would become energized in front of her steady *cantina* audience. She interpreted the snickers and nods from those present to be affirmations of her strength and control, but after a while, the entertainment got stale and the assembled would leave, one by one. Perhaps they became uncomfortable seeing even the *cabron*'s manhood so ruthlessly shredded before their eyes. Maybe it was time to go home to make sure their own domestic order and control would not be slipping away from them. After all, no man wants to be known for dancing to the "hen's singing"; *le canta la gallina* is a taunt that compels a man to feel for his zipper for reassurance.

On the other side of the town square lived Nelson Fulano. He was known for being Tempira's leading authority on the most minute particulars of nearly everyone's whereabouts, with-whom-abouts, and other pertinent (and impertinent) information. Some began calling him the "radio-journalist" because he could provide up-to-the minute bulletins, with constant updates. Nelson built his reputation as an information source by paying exquisite attention to everything. His family's house was strategically situated on the corner nearest one of the entrances from the highway into town. Upon first meeting Nelson, one would take him to be about sixteen. Though actually thirty, he had a voice that still cracked and slipped out of the lower register without warning. There was a line of blondish fuzz, trying to become a mustache, capping his upper lip. He looked slight and sickly with the convex chest of a consumptive, developed from slouching.

Nelson did little odd jobs around town, mostly babysitting or running errands. But his real business was surveillance. He never missed a trick. His eyes dart even as they sparkle. He smiles and chats deferentially, unobtrusive in his friendly questioning until you realize that he is actually collecting information to pass along. "So, where were you today? I didn't see you go out," serves as an opener as one meets him on the street. Or he may happen to be standing at the bus terminal in Liberia or Filadelfia waiting to go home as an incoming bus arrives. Not only would Nelson see who was on the bus, but he would wave enthusiastically so you knew he'd seen you. Timing is important, and his was impeccable. As luck would have it, he might be just outside your gate talking to a neighbor just as you leave in a borrowed car. Or maybe a guest who's had a bit too much to drink comes to the door just as Nelson is on his way back from running an errand. "Nelson says" was an authoritative and oft-quoted eye-witness source for a wide range of happenings: how many were at a funeral or wedding, who wasn't there, who cried at what point in the service, what food was served, who came late, why they came late, who left early, where they went. He also was up on the daily events: who was coming back from San Jose; what time they should be arriving; when the telephone repair serviceman arrived; what time the bus passed to and from Liberia, who got on, and who got off; how many bags they carried; who helped them carry the bags; how far the helper went out of his way to help and how long he may have lingered. It is wrong to assume that merely because Nelson might be out of sight, not sitting in the wooden rocker on the front porch, that his antennae are at rest. He could easily be inside the house, shielded from passersby by a sheer curtain in the living room. His younger sister, Catalina, was also a helpful source of information. And now that many neighbors have telephones, the gathering and reporting mechanisms are enhanced by the electronic grapevine.

Not everyone was sanguine about being the subject of Nelson's reports. One evening, Mariana, one of the teen-age daughters of Nelson's neighbors across the street, was to receive a "*serenata*" from a boy she especially liked. It was quite late at night. No one else was out in the dark, still night except the boys who were very quietly setting up the portable tape player and getting ready to present Mariana her serenade. (Times have really changed from the 1960s, when young men used to serenade a lady by playing guitars and singing romantic tunes. Now they play cassette tapes on boom boxes!) Anyway, as the music began to blare, the boys were ready for the curious Nelson. They were expecting him to be investigating the disturbance from behind the slightly parted curtain. They suddenly turned a giant wide-beam flashlight toward Nelson's window, depriving him of any pleasure he might have derived from learning the identity of the young suitor and his friends.

Mariana's aunt Fini tells this story with great relish, remembering when she herself was a teen-ager and Nelson's father saw her kissing a boy and the next day the whole town knew who had been visiting. So Nelson was part of a long family tradition that a newcomer to town might not be aware of but should be. This seemingly unobtrusive weakling whom one might cruelly liken to a eunuch was a force to contend with. To be fair, it should be said that at times Nelson also transmitted as much helpful information as damaging dirt. And no one really bothered to challenge him perhaps because they recognized that he had so few opportunities for more direct pleasures. News was his gift from heaven. "*Pobrecito,*" they said, "his thrills must be obtained vicariously."

But wait! One day another story circulated that someone had accidentally walked in on a ludicrous scene of unimagined passion. There was skeletally thin Nelson, his meticulous hair totally mussed up as he sank to sublime oblivion between the beefy thighs of 300-pound servant girl named Sonia. Right there in the wooden shed behind the corn bin! This story was told with nasty hilarity and malicious disbelief, but it was one story that Nelson, himself, never verified or sent out on his news wires. After all, his reputation was built on knowing other people's business, not, unlike many other men, boasting about his own.

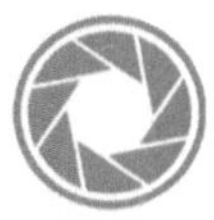

Wide Angle

The Rio Tempisque

If I were making a film at the Tempisque River, I would open with the entire screen filled by a deep mahogany brown pool reflecting ripples and splashes. A large blue dragon fly skims along the surface, its double set of papery wings making a faint clacking sound. As the camera moved back, we would see that the dark brown pool is the watery eye of an ox who is trying to lower his head to take a sip from the river but who is uncomfortably joined to his workmate by a creaking, groaning unpainted yoke. The angles formed by the four curled horns and two heads look totally unnatural, and the grunts and impatient pawing of their unsure footing in the gray sand give the viewer cause to wince. Panning a little further along the shoreline, the camera would slowly take in some milk cows with their young heifers drinking lazily, free of the headgear suffered by their bovine cousins. We would hear in the background a blend of nature's sounds, the cicadas' constant buzz, a woodpecker's hollow tapping, and the chirps, squawks, and varied melodies of enough birds to keep Audubon enthusiasts in ecstasy for hours. Flies of all sizes swim through the air, zipping in circles or lines, but staying within close range of the cows. Graceful, stark white cattle egrets hunker on the wide rumps and rippling shoulders of the cows. They peck at resident ticks and bugs, or simply rest balanced on one spindly leg, eyes closed, in the still, hot air. At dusk as if by some silent signal the entire flock of hundreds will take off together and fly downstream to the large *cenícero* (ash) tree. So many will roost there for the night, that at first glance, the tree will appear to be heavily covered with snow.

The mid-afternoon sky fills with dark clouds accumulating to block out the sun's rays and the remaining blue patches of sky. Thunder can be heard groaning in the distance, far enough away that everyone knows another hour will pass before the much-needed showers arrive. Then, some large leaves from plants growing near the river will come in handy as umbrellas for anyone without a plastic sheet for protection. Every man, at least the older ones, passing by on foot or horseback carries a machete and knows which leaves to cut. They know which don't have hordes of ants crawling on the undersurface at this time of the day and which won't cause a rash if any white ooze from a stem should touch his face.

In the midst of all this pastoral hubbub of wild and domestic creatures, Jose Luis and his brother Jose Antonio are tending the cows for their father, Don Chombo. His real name is Gerónimo, but he likes to be called by his nickname. Chombo ferries workers from the sugarcane fields and processing plant across the river in his *panga*, the dugout boat he made himself. He decided to provide this service when the company began operations and the foot bridge had not yet been built. One year later the newly-built foot bridge was destroyed by the flooded river, so Don Chombo's ferry was still needed. He guides it from a standing position, moving the single, long-handled oar much like a Venetian gondolier. Only three or four men can cross in one trip, so the others wait their turn, smoking cigarettes and leaning against the trees away from the few remaining sunny spots along the shore.

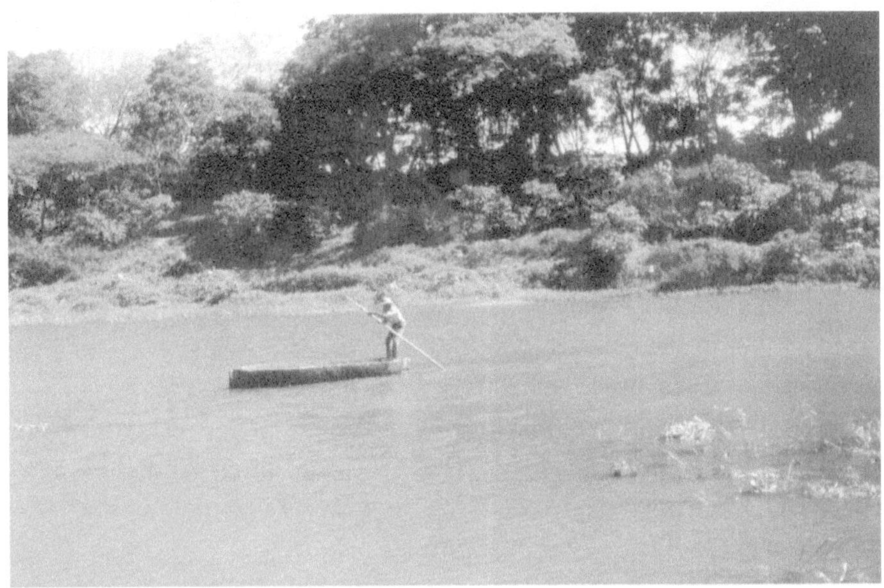

Another day has passed, making it two weeks and two days since the cane cutters had been told their pay might be delayed a few days. Each guards his individual hostility tightly, unwilling to express discontent for fear of being labeled a rabble-rouser or worse yet, a communist. Someone surely would remark to someone else, and word would get back to a foreman with the power to hire and fire. That would mean losing the job, perhaps to a cousin of the one who started the rumor. Those jobs are coveted because the company pays higher wages to *peones* (day laborers) than any other employer in the area. Speaking out might mean being ostracized by the community for not conforming, or appearing ungrateful, or thinking he was better than the rest, or for any number of reasons. Cardinal offenses.

Luis Angel, one of the cane cutters who had worked two seasons in the *bananera,* cutting bananas, near Limon wonders, though, what would happen if they all ganged up on the field manager, if they could ever find him, to demand their money. He never seemed to be where he told them to be to collect their wages, Tuesday at 11 a.m. or Friday at 3 p.m., then most certainly Saturday at noon. This has been going on now for weeks and the men are still guarding their irritation. Luis Angel used to shoot the breeze with some of the *sindicalistas* (union members) in the banana zone. Maybe they could help the cane cutters. Luis Angel keeps the idea to himself, but takes a long last drag on his cigarette before flicking it into the river. He just might make a telephone call tonight. It's hard to live for long on the few *colones* their wives make selling tortillas and corn bread cakes or by washing and ironing clothes for others. The sacks of rice and beans and the five-gallon can of lard will hold out a while longer, but his own extras like *guaro* and cigarettes? So even the *cantina* owners wish these cane cutters would get paid soon, although they are more than willing to extend credit in the meantime.

A raft of water hyacinths with delicate purple flowers floats by. Jose Antonio dives under the gently flowing water, surfacing with wreaths of waxy, green, thick leaves and clusters of hyacinth flowers around his head and shoulders, arms outstretched imitating his idea of the monster from out of the deep.

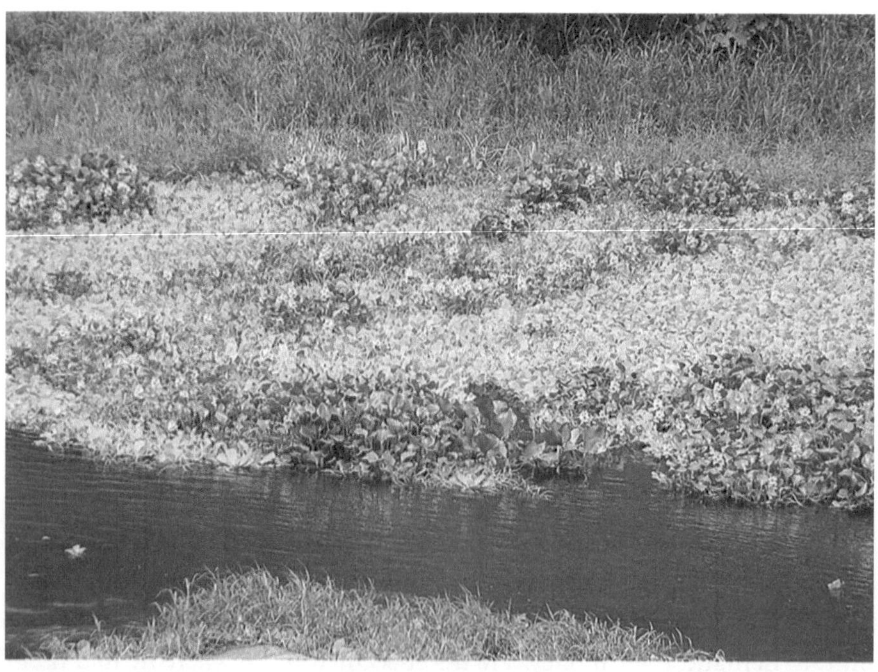

His brother laughs and throws a pebble so it skims across the water. The river is slow and shallow and only about 15 meters wide in late May. The rainy season is just getting underway. By September or October the river's temperament will have altered considerably, becoming torrential and fearsome. Playing in its muddy swirls will be out of the question. For now, though, a handful of nine or ten year old boys on the opposite shore chase a *garrobo* (a kind of iguana).

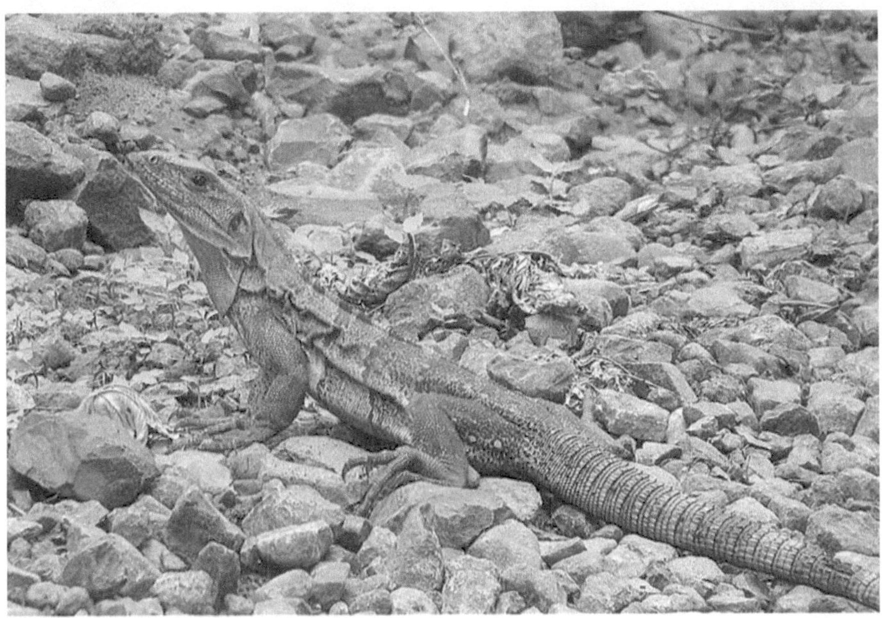

They all scramble up the enormous balsam tree, the boys hugging its smooth barked limbs, moving carefully, and the *garrobo* clamoring rapidly but clumsily, its claws clicking and scratching audibly in the chase. It's hard to know if the *garrobo* is having fun or is terrified. Suddenly they're at the end of the limb with nowhere else to go but down. The lizard tailspins into the water, one or two boys cannonballing right after it. The *garrobo* escapes, and the boys swim and splash each other. They hoot and yip, miniatures of their fathers and older brothers who make similar sounds in the *cantina* or at the bull riding events during *fiestas*.

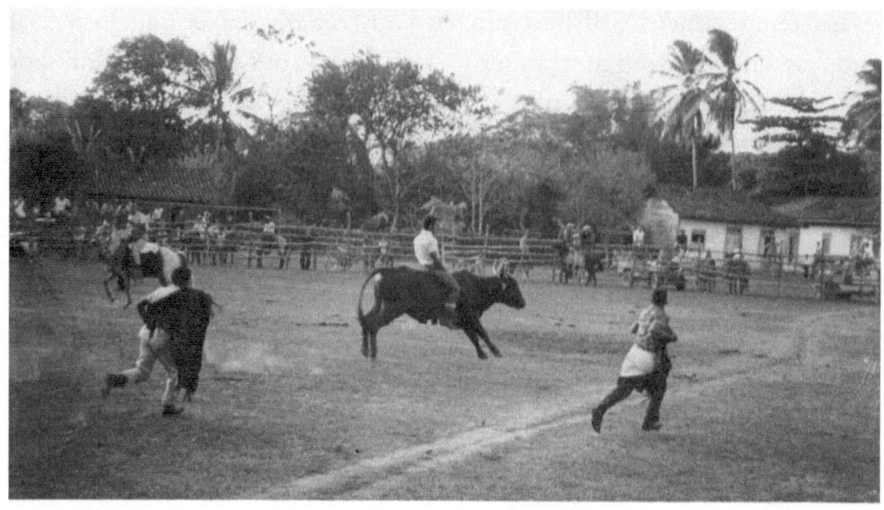

In nearby trees along the river, families of *congos* (Howler monkeys), lounge placidly, draping their bodies over the limbs. A mama *congo* with her baby clinging to her back changes locations to reach for some fresh leaves. The large old granddads and younger males just seem literally to "hang out" in the same spot for hours. Occasionally they are moved to engage in some deep baritone howling, imitatable by a human who draws inward in short breaths, "Uwwuu-uuu-uuu-uuuuuuuu."

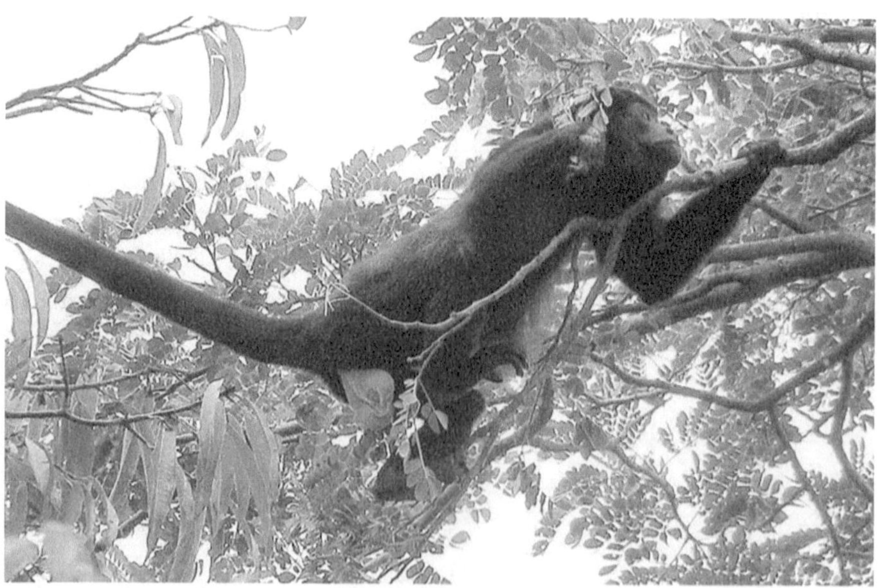

Downstream from this game of *garrobo* tag (or is it torture?), Constanza, Tancha for short, stands thigh-deep in the water. Never married and around forty-five, she is the aunt of one of the boys frolicking in the water. She is bent over her favorite flat rock on the river's edge, finishing the laundry that she, Rocio, and Arlen, her sister's teenage daughters, had been at all afternoon. It is hard to ignore the noise the boys and the monkeys create. Yet all these sounds are part of the completely natural scene. Constanza wants to get home before the showers arrive. She and the girls had been there for hours, assiduously scrubbing each blouse, towel, or blue jean, first rubbing the bar of blue laundry soap over the entire surface, then scooping water up in a gourd bowl to make the soap lather up. The girls helped lay the clothes out or hang them on nearby bushes to dry but left Constanza to finish alone. They had to get back to help their *'buelita* (*abuelita*, grandmother) with the late afternoon chores, sweeping the yard, feeding the chickens, and bathing their baby brother, Ivan. Every now and then Constanza stands and leans backward to flex her aching back. She yells sharply at the boys to be careful, fixing her gaze on their tireless play. At the same time she chips off bits of the soap bar with her nails to try to distract the annoying *sardinas* (little fish) nipping at her legs like tiny pinpricks. Her laundering spot is conveniently located near where Don Chombo beaches his *panga*, and Constanza wonders if there still might be a chance for her to enjoy a little romantic pleasure with him even though his dark skin looks gray and cracked like an old leather *albarda*, and his smile is more gummy than toothy. She glances sideways, respositioning her back so he'll notice her as the boat approaches. The guys in the *panga* also notice her subtle shift and begin to tease and taunt, *"Ay, mira Chombito, mira la lavanderota, jueputa, parece que te tiene un regalo, cabrón!"* [!*] Usually taciturn and kindly, Don Chombo grumbles, and Constanza pretends to be indignant and vigorously swings her scrubbing arm outward as if brushing at a bothersome fly with the back of her hand. "Ach, you're a bunch of *necios, molestones* (bothersome pains in the neck) all of you. *Dejen de joder!"* (Quit messing around!)

None of these people is a stranger to any other. They've all lived their entire lives in this town, dodging each others' gossip and taunts,

---

* Hey, Chombo, look at the big washerwoman, sonofabitch, looks like she has a gift for you, you old goat!

aware of every newcomer in town from the occasional dry goods salesmen to Spanish priests to school teachers from the Central Valley to the American Peace Corps volunteer. But as Don Chombo once reflected, all the outsiders eventually leave. Those born and raised here have lived each other's flirtations and rejections, survived each other's unpaid loans and unreturned favors, shared each other's illnesses. They know who's to be trusted or not, and who can fix or make any item, from tractors to brooms. They remember the night that Miguelito was fatally hit on his bicycle by Edwin from another town, who was driving drunk in his fancy new pickup truck. They remember how Edwin gave up drinking then but only had to pay a shamefully modest fine because his father was a big deal in the *Liberacion* party. They put a white cross marker with some plastic roses on the side of the road to help remember that spot. They know how many children old Sanchez has fathered with how many women in the area. They know and remember volumes that have never been written down. And, when all is said and done, they will recite each others' funeral rosaries and walk together behind the caskets to the cemetery. They still half joke about the time they were forced to move the cemetery. One year during an especially fierce rainy season the river overflowed its banks and flooded the cemetery. Caskets were unearthed, frightening and sickening the neighbors and drawing the attention of all the dogs in town. A team of townsmen quickly acted to re-inter the caskets with bodies in various stages of decomposition. They built cement casings above ground under the direction of Don Martin, the carpenter and cement mason. Blocks of beehive-like structures now stand, some with statues of angels or covered with pastel pink or white glazed ceramic tiles. At various times of the year family members adorn the graves with vases or wreaths of Easter lilies, roses, and other flowers made from silk and wire and sold by Doña Elena. She's the bar owner's wife in the next town who has turned her hobby into a good business.

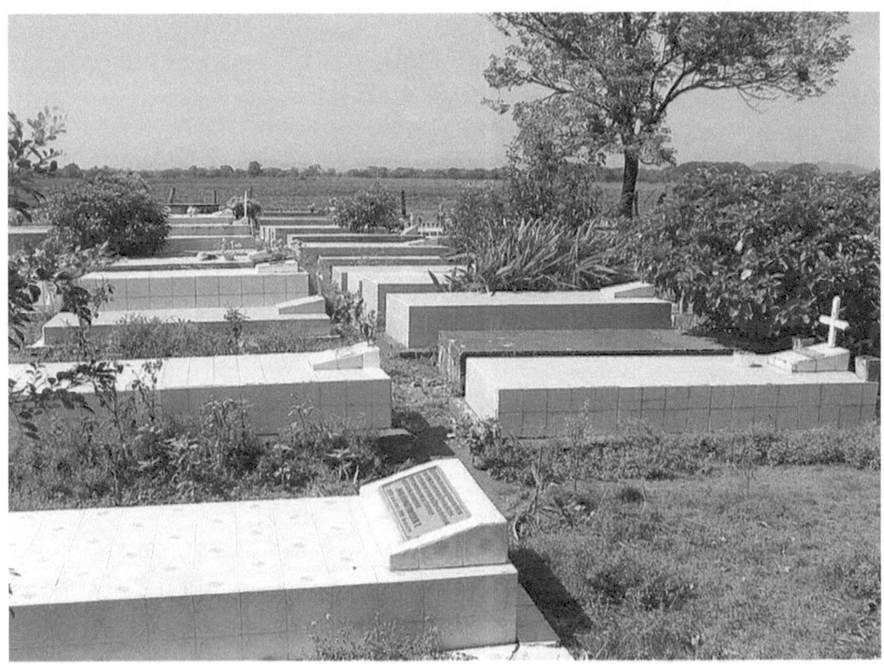

They also will remember each other with rosary gatherings, special masses and notices in the paper every year on the anniversary of a death. There is no doubt in their minds that this is where each of them will ultimately end up. They will be laid to rest near their mother who died at fifty-five after toiling to raise fourteen children; and their brother who was gored by the bull as everyone gasped in horror during the church fiesta to raise funds; and their uncle who developed cancer after years of mixing insecticides for the local crop dusting enterprise. And they know they will not be the last to rest there. There will those who come after them, an infant nephew who will die of gastroenteritis, a daughter who develops peritonitis after a Caesarian, or a son who loses control of his Yamaha100 *moto* (motorbike) after too many ice cold Pilsens.

They suspect they are locked into eternity together, so why not joke and tease and flirt and lust and laugh while they can?

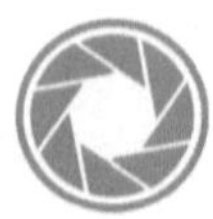

Animation

Kids' Morning

As the early morning sun cast its not yet so hot rays on the dusty roadway in front of the house, eight year-old Jesus leaned on the wooden doorsill munching a warm tortilla folded over and filled with last night's rice and beans. On his shoulder, gently clutching his tee shirt in its fist-like claws sat a bright green and turquoise parakeet, contentedly sharing a bean morsel and expressing his greedy delight by squawking "*Deme mas, urrrrria, periquito.*" (Gimme more, urrrrrria little parrot) Cesar, Jesus' twin, was rubbing the sleep from his eyes as he sat down on the doorstep waiting for Jesus to finish.

A pink pig browsed selectively through a pile of garbage at the edge of the street. Deciding on a large piece of watermelon rind, he squoinked as he nuzzled the juiceless scrap. Even the wire ring through his nose didn't prevent his muzzling into the pale dusty roadside.

Jesus shoved the last bite into his mouth and tugged at Cesar's shirt. Together with the mounted parakeet they galloped and squealed, surprising the pig from both sides and accompanying him at full speed down the middle of the street. The pig looked uncomfortable, running as though it wore high-heeled shoes, the pounds of lard jiggling under its ribs. The squawks of the parakeet, the squeals of the pig, and screaming hoots of the boys blended into a cacophony of non-musical disharmony. So concentrated on their pig-chasing mission, Jesus and Cesar didn't even look up when they passed their *abuelita* (grandmother). She was returning to their house after completing her daily task of taking a pitcher of milk to her other son's wife who, two weeks before, had given birth to their third child.

Abuelita's tall, angular, bony frame stooped slightly forward as she scuffed along, her long gray braids hanging limply and her very-bowed legs jutting at irregular angles through her pink cotton frock. Abuelita barely noticed that it was her grandsons who were making such a scandal chasing that pig. She looked tired, even before the day got started. Her work in the dirt-floored kitchen was waiting, as it had waited for her every other morning: grinding corn for tortillas in the hand-turned metal grinder hooked to the table edge; sorting grains of rice from the pebbles and chaff for the day's potful; salting the bowl of meat so it wouldn't spoil during the heat of the morning. Alicia, her daughter-in-law and mother of the twins, tried her best to stay clear of those household chores. Her pretty face gave her pretensions of cover-girl glamour, and she spent hours putting on make-up and fixing her hair and nails. She'd arrive in the kitchen once all the corn had been ground, and the beans and rice were already cooking atop the flat lime-covered wood-fueled stove. *Abuelita* could only dream of having a *muchacha* who could come in and help her with the chores for a few hours each day. It certainly was not going to be the glamour queen!

In mid-April dust was everywhere, swirling in powdery eddies whenever a truck or jeep rumbled through town or if an occasional breeze blew. Dust baked onto one's sweat-moistened face and caked gritty layers on newly waxed floors, under the bedcover edges, inside any open crevice. When will the welcome first rains begin? It's almost May, shouldn't be too much longer. That first rain always seems so tentative, but even a little rain would placate the dust, each droplet forming a little indentation one by one until a dark moist layer of dust weighed down on the rest. The smell of that first rain on the dryness is unlike any other. But more than the welcome smell, the first rains bring hope that there will be food, thus life, for another year. *Abuelita* may have been a tired old lady who seldom smiled, but she was looking forward to her seventy-second "first" rain shower. That wonderful smell of the wet dust that only happens after the first rain!

Carrying the empty, green plastic milk pitcher, *Abuelita* stopped to see what was going on in the churchyard to her right. She peered through the rusty barbed wire fence at the pair of yoked oxen waiting to work.

One, sprawled on the ground, nonchalantly chewed his cud, while the other kneeled next to him, twisting his head in the yoke, looking for a few moist morsels among the wheat-colored weeds. Don Pedro, *Abuelita*'s husband, got the cart ready while Alejandro, the twins' father, entered the churchyard to lead the oxen through the gate to the cart in the street. "*Huweya*" he practically coughed to stir the oxen as he prodded and poked them with a metal-tipped stick. They dutifully stood up, unfolding their clumsy legs to rise. The old wooden yoke, with chips of blue-green paint still visible, creaked solidly as the beasts moved their haunches. After a few attempts at rebellion, butting each other with their great curved horns, the pair seemed to resign themselves to the day's work ahead and docilely lowered their heads as Alejandro and Don Pedro hitched them to the *carreta*. The two men threw in their shovels and were now set for the walk to the river where they would load sand for mixing with cement. They needed to have it all ready for Martin, the carpenter, who was building an addition onto their house.

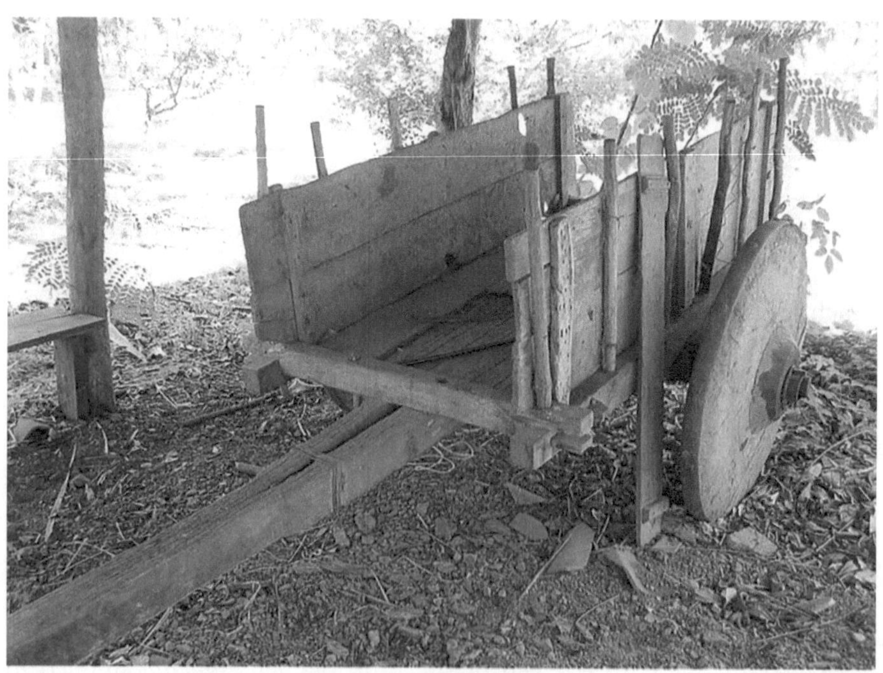

Meanwhile Jesus and Cesar, from halfway around the plaza, abandoned the pig that stood panting and snorting near a pile of leaves that the *Guardia Rural* (local cop) had swept away from the doorway of his post. The twins spotted the *Niña* (Miss) Elvia, their teacher, talking to a neighbor outside her house. They raced home to shower, put on their regulation blue shorts, white shirts, and black socks and shoes, and comb their straight black hair. School would begin at 7:00, and if the *Niña* was already on her way, that didn't leave them much time to get cleaned and polished.

From a short distance, the strains of national anthem could be heard, as the thirty other school children stood in the open corridor of the three-room schoolhouse. "*Noble Patria, tu hermosa bandera, expresion de tu vida nos da. . .* " Jesus and Cesar, scrubbed and ready for another day slipped into line and joined the singing without missing a beat "*. . .bajo el limpido azul de tu cielo, blanca y pura descansa la paz.*"

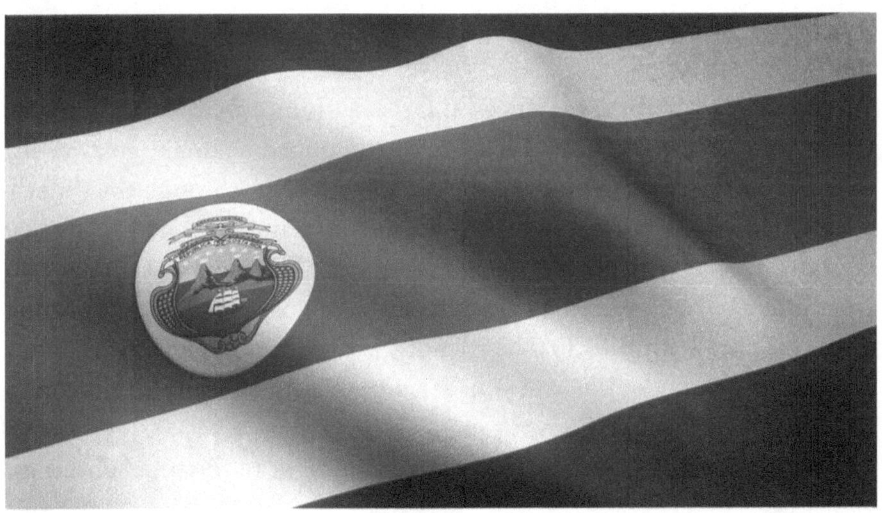

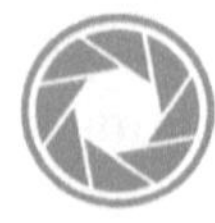

Pura Película

Armando

I heard the crunching gravel under the horse's hooves as he rode into the yard. Then the sounds of the creaking leather *albarda* and the impatient pawing and equine snorts of his horse as it made abrupt turns and stops. There was something threatening in the nearness of such a strong animal.

Seven years had passed since I'd last seen him, when I was the Peace Corps volunteer in Tempira. I felt scared and hoped he might go away if I didn't go to the door. I could see the sleek black horse through the slightly open faded yellow curtain and then heard the heavy clunk of his cowboy boots as he stepped onto the green tiled porch. Why not just go out and greet him as I had greeted all the rest of the townspeople since returning to Guanacaste with Bill? Just be friendly, polite, indifferent.

"*Hola*, Armando, how are you? It's nice to see you again," I faked.

"Is he your husband or your man?"

No hello, no how are you. He was getting right to the heart of things, wasn't he?

I lied, "He's my husband."

"Are you sure you're not lying? Is he your husband or your man?"

"What difference could it possibly make? I am with him."

Besides, where did this possessiveness come from? I was never "his" despite whatever had happened.

How he had aged in those seven years! Though he was only in his early thirties, his thick hair was noticeably graying. The years of binge drinking had given his eyes a strange glassy blur. Still, I was drawn to this stereotype of a Guanacaste cowboy, tough, muscular, bronzed, fearless, raw, virile. Years ago, I thought I could save him from himself, give him courage to stop drinking, convince him of the dangers, all those *cliches* that a well-meaning, naive, idealistic *gringa* could dream up. A real project with a humane purpose. Sigh.

When I first met him, I was too repressed and uninitiated even at twenty-two to be conscious of the carnality that was this man's stock in trade: his deep copper chest that showed under the shirt unbuttoned nearly to his waist; his thick, blue-jeaned thighs; his square, strong working hands; and the one slightly tilted eyebrow over his deep brown, fiery eyes. Mando had a way of making women feel uneasy by staring, asking a direct question, and biting his gold front tooth as he waited for a reply.

I recalled when he first came out of the *cantina* to meet me. I had moved to Tempira only a few days earlier and was out walking alone in the afternoon sun. He approached me and began walking down the street with me. Gripping my upper arm, then tightly holding my wrist, the smell of liquor on his breath, he invited, then urged, then pleaded with me to go to the movies with him. I had been brought up to be polite no matter what, and no one had ever laid a hand on me in a way so aggressive. It both scared and fascinated me. Standing in the middle of the street with this stranger, I refused his "kind" invitation, thank you, but I would not be going to the movies with him. He stared at me but loosened his grip on my wrist. I was immediately conscious of neighbors' eyes and later the tales that would be set in motion by this little scene. I'd already been in Latin America for over a year and was not ignorant of how a girl's virtue is evaluated. They'd be thinking that if I allowed him to touch my arm in public, then we must have already established a more intimate understanding in private. I didn't want to offend him, but I feared for my good-girl reputation. It had never occurred to me before going to Costa Rica that people could make so much of two people talking in the street, even if they had been flirting, which I wasn't. Maybe he also read more into my politeness, mistaking it for encouragement, even though I had refused to go to the movies with him. Was he seeing this "no thank you" as a temporary setback on the road to "*conquista*"?

In the sheltered family and world that I'd grown up in in the 1950s and 1960s, raw sexuality was not in every TV advertisement or movie, or popular song lyric the way it is today. Young girls exposed to this now grow up knowing what's what very early on. (I was so stupidly innocent that I thought the fig leaf covering male statue's private parts was actually a flap of skin that was part of their anatomy! Imagine the shock.). So I was not prepared for the attentions and the apparent intentions of this near-caricature of virile energy.

He started to bring me gifts: a conch shell, which he himself had loosened from a reef after swimming hundreds of feet in *Bahia de Culebra*. Another time he said he wanted me to have a *recuerdo* (souvenir) of the *Pampa Guanacasteca* and gave me his machete in a tooled leather sheath along with a hollowed-out cow horn fashioned into a container for carrying *carbolina* (carbolic acid) used for cleaning out ticks and bat bites in horses and cattle. Another time he gave me a gold medallion of *La Virgen de Los Angeles* (the patron saint of Costa Rica) and insisted that, in the spirit of fairness, I let him hold my silver filigree *mezuzah* in return. When I asked for it back after a few minutes, he refused, clutching it to his heart, begging to keep it as a *recuerdo* of me. I figured he'd given me all these things so the least I could do was let him keep the *mezuzah.* Maybe I even had some warped notion of it promoting ecumenical balance. Then he used to bring me soda pop from the *cantina*, and he would put *pesetas* (25 cent coins) into the *rocola* (from rockola, the jukebox) to play songs he dedicated to me, Magda, the *cantinera* would tell me later. Songs about being "a prisoner of love," "writing love letters in blood," and "never returning because you've rejected me." She seemed to take a conspiratorial interest trying to convince me that he was a great guy and really was lovesick over me!

I did not know how to handle these gestures, but my girl friends and their father, Don Alberto, always told me not to look at him and warned me against responding with more than formal politeness. There is no such thing as a school-boy crush or an "innocent movie date" He knew Mando's intentions were much more than I was prepared for or could even imagine. I just thought someone liked me. By accepting his little gifts and even continuing to speak with him when he showed up, however, I was already allowing him (and the world!) to build more into the "relationship" than I knew.

Most people in town found Armando a show-off, *pura pelicula* and most everyone could give vivid detailed descriptions of his latest "performance," usually one soaked in alcohol. They liked to tell about the times he wildly rode his horse Midnight down the street wearing a colorful Mexican *serape* over his shoulder and a giant black velvet, souvenir *charro* hat on his head, one hand holding it on.

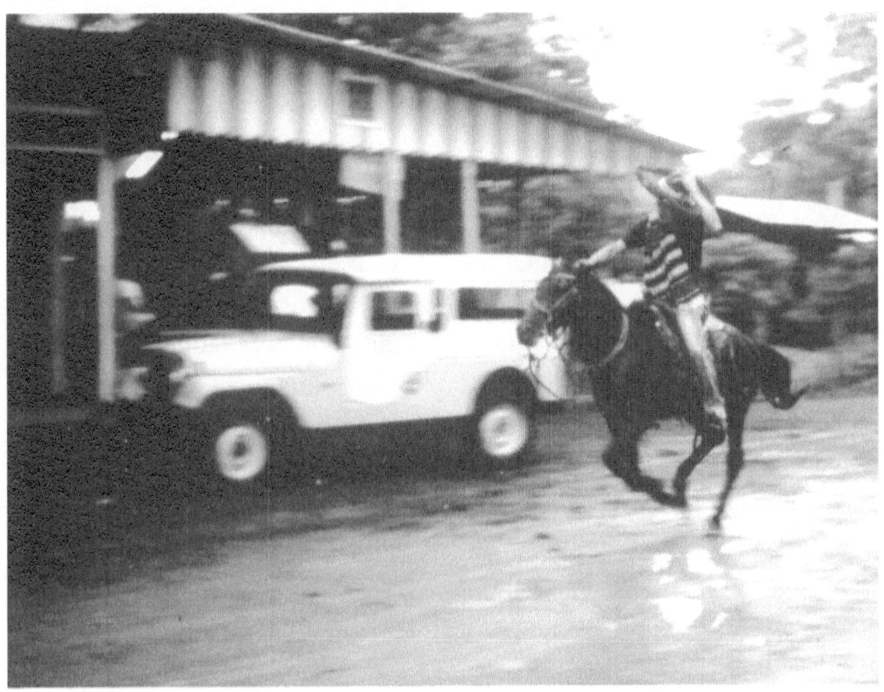

He would whoop and hoot, forcing the horse to stop and go, rear up or turn abruptly, then prance parade style, paw the street, then turn and take off running again, leaving eddies of dust in his wake. Mothers would frantically call children off the street. Frightened old people knew to move well out of his way. Nearby neighbors closed the wooden shutters of their windows, content to watch the action safely between the gaps in the wooden wall boards. Mando's godfather, Don Alberto would look worriedly through the dining room screen, tsk-tsking his disapproval of his godson's out-of-control behavior. He and Mando's father, Don Daniel, had been close friends all their lives. "Whatever had gone wrong with that boy?" he would ask, knowing the answer in his heart, knowing that his friend's home was violent and intimidating. Mando and his older brother, Danielillo, were Don Daniel's two eldest sons in a family of twelve, Both sons had serious problems with their father whom they were forced to respect even while watching him yell at or smack their mother in the face. When they would rise up against him to defend their mother, he would beat them with his wide leather belt.

Drinking was at the heart of it all. It was at first a way to muffle the painful truth of what they had witnessed at home and to prove their own manliness in the face of such powerlessness. Perhaps it was a way to divert their father's attention with misbehavior so he would stop abusing their mother. As the boy who managed to get through to the 6th grade turned into an adolescent who wanted to be a man before his time, Mando found a home in the *cantina*. There he got respect, real or fake, from the *sabaneros* (cowhands) and *peones* (field laborers) because he was their *patron*'s son. It was a fair trade and an easy route to the free drinks which Mando bought for them. That way of life, day in and day out, was launched a decade before I ever knew about Costa Rica, let alone imagined ever going there. At the age of sixteen, Mando had run off with the young house servant, three years his senior, against his parents' desire (or perhaps because of their opposition). At twenty-four he was already the father of four, not counting others scattered around Guanacaste with other mothers. Lots of women were more than eager to have one of Mando's children and have some link to his prosperous family. But these were not girls from "respectable" families.

What I thought I saw in my do-gooder mind, was a troubled young man who just needed to be introduced to the possibility of change and life goals. With missionary zeal, I used every opportunity when he came near me to talk to him about Alcoholics Anonymous, to tell him the reasons he should stop drinking and on and on, in ways that wanting-to-be-helpful-females try to cajole and persuade people they care about to stop drinking. If only he would stop drinking, so went my well-intentioned litany, everything else would straighten out. (What all the "everything else" was, I was not sure.) He probably didn't care what I was talking about as long as I was paying attention to him. The *gringa* was talking to him and not to someone else!

Armando's drinking bouts could go on indefinitely—a weekend, four days, two weeks. He was incapable of having just one or two drinks and moving on. He would drop into Magda's *cantina*, slip some *pesetas* into the giant Wurlitzer jukebox with its swirling colors, order a drink and soon all the hangers-on in the *cantina* would come around, hoping that Mando would invite them for the next round. He was like a magnet, everyone wanting to slap his shoulder in greeting and flatter him in return for just one *traguito* (little drink). Occasionally, after many hours of drinking, Mando would give his stuporous audiences the real stuff of legends. He'd whip out his .22 pistol with the mother-of-pearl handle, aim at and shoot a few bottles behind the bar, evoking half-angry screams and goading laughter from Magda, who indulged his excesses and excused his behavior. After all, deep down Mando was a good, though misguided, fellow and no one really to be afraid of, just a little out of control. Just a boy being a boy, after all, she would say afterwards.

"Mando, what are you doing, are you *crazy? Deja. hombre.* (That's enough.) Now, go over there and sit down, I'll bring you a little something to eat." Yet another "mommy" whose attention he garnered and devoured.

He would push the pistol back into his hip holster and stagger over to a table, sometimes knocking over one of the low green stools in his path, and lay his head down while waiting to be served. Along with the plate of food, Magda also made sure to bring him a double *guiski* and some water for a chaser, as she kept a running tally of his expenses, including the bottles he'd shot off the wall. Mando was always good for business.

Young boys hiding outside the cantina watching all this would spread the word quickly, "Mando's shooting bottles of *guaro*!" The excitement was energizing and filled them with admiration. This was live TV before television ever reached Tempira! When he finally got ready to leave or was kicked out of the cantina, he'd stumble over to where his patient and faithful steed, Midnight, stood hitched. He used to say that his horse was the only faithful being in his life, the only one he could really trust. After a couple of stumbling attempts to get on the horse, he would finally make it and take off running to the other *cantina* around the corner. Sometimes, still seated on the horse, he'd lean inside the window and ask for a drink. Other times, he'd dismount, steady himself at the doorway and proceed to the bar and order up another double. Fast as flies attracted to dog shit, one or two field hands would amble over and drape themselves on his neck in the embrace of fast friends bending elbows in unholy communion.

It was not unusual in those days of insatiable thirst to find Mando asleep in the corner of the cantina or in the doorway, even though his house was only a half-mile up the road. One Sunday morning, after a Saturday night dance at Magda's, just past dawn, a jeep from the *comandancia* (command post) in Liberia pulled up to the cantina, and two uniformed *guardias* got out and sauntered over to where Mando was lying curled in the cantina doorway. They roused him by bumping a billy club on his butt. He raised his head slowly and groggily, looking suspiciously at the two policemen. He rubbed his hair with two hands, blew his nose, and spit dryly to remove the foul taste from his mouth. Head hanging, and using the wall of the cantina to help him keep his balance, he managed to get to his feet; but when they moved to handcuff him, he fell to one side, rolling over and kicking to keep them from touching him. As he tried to get away, the cops surrounded him and grabbed his wrists and ankles, tying him up like a calf being taken for branding, and literally threw him, hogtied, into the back of the jeep.

As all that was happening, I was eating breakfast with Don Alberto's daughters half a block away and could see, along with the rest of the village by this time, what was going on. Why had the police come from Liberia, and why were they taking him away like an animal, obliterating even further any remote sense of dignity after his night of *borrachera* (drunken partying)? He was so obviously in a fog, barely focusing on the morning and probably only vaguely able to remember the night before. Or could he?

Ah yes, the night before, he and his brother Danielillo had paid the *marimberos* (the four guys who play the marimba) to move their giant wooden xylophone-like instrument across the street to serenade the *gringuita* (me) who lived there.

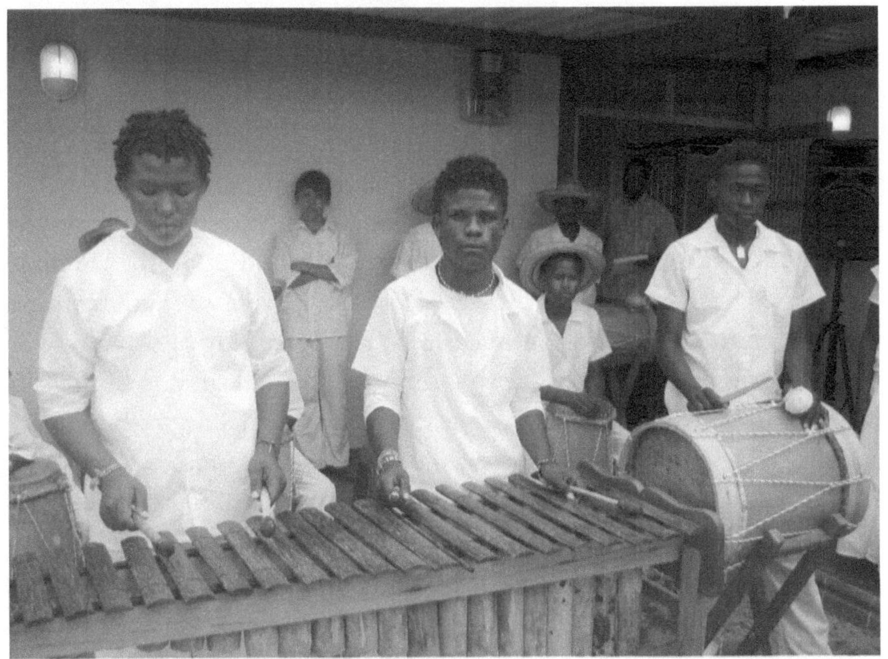

And as they were playing and singing at 2:00 in the morning, the local rural *guardia*, Don Pinche, who happened to be a member of the political party opposed to the one Don Daniel and his family belonged to, came by to shut down this sentimental enterprise. His real name was Rómulo, but his nickname was Don Pinche because he was so stingy and had beady little eyes and loved to taunt Don Daniel and his sons with the fact that *Liberacion Nacional* no longer was in power, and now he and his party ruled the roost. And his word was the law now, *carajo*! and **he** had decided that they were making a civil disturbance and would have to pack up and go home.

Don Pinche was a slightly built man with a bony face that rarely smiled. Here he was confronting Danielillo and Armando who were feeling like celebrating and singing love songs to the strains of the *marimba*. They were in an expansive, melancholy mood, yet happy in their *macho* attempt to let the *gringuita* know of Armando's unrequited ardor. Don Pinche was running out of patience. As he tried once again to stop the serenade and moved closer to Danielillo, he felt a closed his fist on his jaw, not hard enough to make him fall, but hard enough to get the offender for hitting a lawman. Don Pinche only needed a tiny excuse to exercise the power of his badge. By then the *marimberos* were giving each other concerned let's-pack-up-and-get-out-of-here looks. Silence fell on the whole company. Don Pinche went away vowing to get even, and Danielillo took off in his jeep for Fini's house at the end of the street, leaving Armando to pay the *marimberos* and go off into the night, alone with Midnight, looking for another drink. He was all of a sudden very thirsty. But all the cantinas were closed by now, so he just hunkered against the doorway at the cantina across from the *plaza,* soon falling asleep. The next thing he was aware of was being awakened by the *guardias* from Liberia and finding himself in the jeep on his way to the *cuartel,* the dank, stinking jail in the provincial garrison. Just outside the door stood the placid-looking statue of *La Virgen de los Angeles* benevolently radiating from her raised, pink ceramic niche with gold and orange marigolds planted around its base. (Today the *Antigua comandancia* stands as a museum in Liberia, the statue of the *Virgen* removed.)

I felt a combination of sympathy and guilt for what I saw as my being the cause for the series of unfortunate events. That, plus a curious, unexplainable fascination compelled me to go to Liberia the next day to visit Mando in the *cuartel.* My visit, I reasoned, would acknowledge my appreciation for the aborted serenade and let him know that I felt bad about this indignity, and more, this injustice he was suffering in place of his brother who was the one who had punched Don Romulo. I was nervous about seeing him. I had never been near, let alone in, a jail, nor known anyone who had been incarcerated. I wondered if he would be chained to a wall of a dungeon-like cell. It never occurred to me that anyone else would see me go there. Although I was jittery inside, I tried to put on a very brave, nonchalant exterior, as though it were the most natural thing in the world for a young North American girl to be knocking on the enormous steel door of the provincial garrison, *la comandancia*, asking to see one of the detainees.

The guards must have been surprised to see the likes of me in my white Peter Pan blouse, green wrap-around skirt, and white tennis shoes. They even let me in without asking to see any identification or searching me or anything. They led me to the top of the narrow stairway leading down to the courtyard where the prisoners were lounging around, smoking cigarettes and talking quietly among themselves. At once, they all turned their attention to me, and I froze in embarrassment. There was Mando, still in his dust-stained blue Wranglers and the tan shirt that had been ripped at the shoulder during the struggle when the police had bound him to cart him off. I know he saw me because he turned away abruptly and began to cough, breaking the silence that had overtaken the place. He turned back towards me and raised his pinky in a sort of wave, and bowed his head into his knees. I turned swiftly to leave, embarrassed by having mortified him by seeing him like that. I left the *cuartel* with great remorse, thanking the guard perfunctorily. I felt relieved to be outside the walls where I could see people lining up to get on the bus, carrying bundles and babies from the market just across the street. The day was stiflingly muggy, and the clouds were building up to rain. On the bumpy bus trip back down the unpaved highway, I stared out the window as the rain began pelting the rocks on the side of the road. My vision blurred as tears welled up in my eyes. When I went back to Tempira, I told Mando's younger brother and sister that I had seen him, but I didn't tell anyone else.

Maybe it was still out of guilt for all that had happened that, several weeks later, I was convinced that Mando was sincere when he said he would go to AA in San Jose but only if I would go along with him. Could it be that I'd really gotten him to that point of wanting to stop drinking? He went to San Jose, and I went several days later. We had agreed to meet early in the morning on the steps of the AA house on the *Paseo Colon* in the center of the city. When we went into the office, the man at the desk asked Mando a few questions about his drinking habits. Since Mando was sober at the time, the man concluded the interview in short order, determining that Mando didn't really have much of a drinking problem, or if he did, he should return when he was drunk. I was thoroughly dejected and outraged at that reaction. After all those months of trying to get him to go to AA and that was the professional response? That he didn't really have a problem. Poof, no problem!

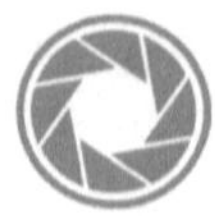

Unbalanced Composition

Getting Married

Journal entry-February, 1974

The cool, night air brushed my cheeks as I lay in the hammock watching Bill. Standing with one leg on a chair, or now and then walking around, he concentrated his gaze as he picked out the intricate patterns on his guitar. Tears glistened in his blue eyes. The high half moon lighted the sky and his face as he sang a mournful cowboy song, not out of place in Guanacaste. The night, however, was not silently listening to his deep, sweet voice. He was accompanied by a droning cow from the pasture behind the house. A chorus of roosters from all around the small town took turns cock-a-doodling solos round-robin style, first a near one, then one a little further down the road, then one way far away, and back to the near one again. The creaking limbs of the nearby coyol tree and the lisping of the drying banana leaves offered light background percussion to the soft guitar melody. Out of the dark blue shadows whirred a large bat, the only creature around that seemed to be rushing somewhere. Bill's face reflected the blue-white pallor of the moonlight. His Kenny-Rogers-like voice was soft and soothing. He was singing about being a "rambling man." The words were always the hard part for me to listen to. Have I tried to trap the wind? I'll always remember that moonlight on his face.

Journal entry two weeks later:

Wouldn't you know? I waited all month to see the rising of the full moon and I missed it, merely because I was absorbed in the newspaper as I lay in the hammock. By the time I looked up it had already risen above the tree tops. When it's at the horizon it's as orange as a ripe persimmon but now it had paled.

The evening is cool, and there's a strong breeze. I have to fold the newspaper pages to keep them blowing. A man-made satellite cruises across the darkening sky. Sometimes I wonder about my ability to feel as deeply as I did when I was younger. I'm only 31 but it feels old. (My father always said that he married my mother at 24 and saved her from spinsterhood, and every year after I was 24 was just another year deeper into spinsterhood.) I'm not so willing to put myself on the line so freely as I once did. One of the Fulano girls a little older than me asked why I was so disillusioned with life. What a long story I'd have to tell her. Can I turn into a person who won't feel because it hurts? I sometimes wonder where each day is taking me, but if I think about it too much I get depressed and feel useless. Better to live each day and not think about the long term. Living each day has one big advantage: I don't have to justify my existence. I don't have to define my "purpose in life." Let's see, today I lived to: fix breakfast, sweep the floor, cook some rice, write a letter to my parents, crochet three rows on a rug, fix lunch, go into town, call the lawyer about some papers, take some pictures of some pink blossoms against the blue sky, talk to Magda, the cantinera, who believes that whatever happens to Guanacaste in the future will be guided by God. What else did I "accomplish" today? I played with the parrots, took a shower, read the newspaper, and missed the moon's rising. Pretty soon Bill will be back and I'll fix supper. He doesn't kiss me or hug me anymore. He did apologize for yelling at me yesterday, about something I'd even forgotten, that's how little I'm beginning to feel things. I come from a family of yelling, so it doesn't even seem out of the ordinary. Silence is what strikes terror. He says he cares; I don't really know why. He's got ideas about "rambling, "sailing, being alone. He says he cares about me but can't give me support and is too close everyday to be able to give demonstrable affection. I often wonder if he cares, but he says he does. I often wonder what I'm giving him, and I wonder what he thinks he's giving me. I can't think about being with another because he's comfortable, but a little hug or spontaneous kiss now and then would feel even more comfortable.

Your presence surrounds me
And sometimes I feel loving
Your presence surrounds me
And sometimes I feel stifled.
Your presence surrounds me
Even when you 're not present.

So here we are.
Where?
So that's it?
What?
So now you know?
Why?
I'll see you.
When?
But that's how it is.
How?
But how can that be?
IT JUST IS !!
What should I do?
Easy. **Live or die.**

Journal entry a week later:

The dog next door is barking monotonously to the accompanying constant buzz of cicadas. The air is stifling hot, at least from inside the house where there is no breeze. The bare yellow light bulb hanging from the ceiling casts the shadow of my hand on top of the space I'm writing in. Moods are bad in this heat. The prospect of sleeping in that tiny bed together is not inviting in such heat. There's always the chill of the morning air to look forward to, I suppose. The small insects tonight are bothersome. How easy it is to snuff out such a life, just with the rub of a thumb, or a handclap. Bill has gone out. I watched him putting on a clean shirt and dabbing on aftershave lotion. It's hard not to figure out that he's going over to see HER. I must try to concentrate on other thoughts.

Yes, think about the garzas (white cattle egrets) at sundown as they fly overhead in small groups of three or four, the wind draughts guiding their flight. They flap their wings in almost perfect unison and stop flapping at the same time, as though a leader were counting out a marking pattern: flap, flap, flap, glide, flap, flap, flap, glide. Military jet squadrons aim to imitate for this graceful precision. Look, there's one bird out alone, away from the flock.

Long slender bird, where are you flying, all alone in the twilight, sailing high and gently in the warm breeze? Are you going home to roost for the night, or are you just out for a little "after-dinner stroll"?

Think about Bill's mother. You know what I like about your mother? She always sends her love to us both and I feel like she means it.

Somedqy high tide will carry you away from me.
But tides come back into shore,
And the shore is most always there,
just as surely as the sea is, and I am not afraid.
I stay caught up in the beauty and the fury,
the storm and the calm, the constancy that I love.
I need a project. I need to know you care.

Journal entry, three weeks later, a note to Bill.

I'll ask you again since I asked you last night when you were drunk and/or half asleep and I can't be sure of your answer: By your definition, are you and I having an affair?

STOP TO ANSWER BEFORE READING ON.

Is that really how you think of it? As a fleeting romantic encounter that is pleasant to recall, but destined to nothingness by its very definition? Affair implies ending right from the beginning. If that's how you think, we might as well end it now rather than drag it out, get on with your other brief encounters, the weekend fury with someone you may never see again, the detached convenience that makes you sad for a day or two when it's over, but always ready to move on. Ah, the rambling man, like the wind, like the tides.

I resent your calling what you had for five years with Linda an affair. But I resent even more that you would call your time with me an affair. I have given you my heart. Doesn't that count for something? Doesn't an affair need two people to agree that it's an affair?

I cannot share myself and my life with someone who can be so facile about calling my love and friendship "an affair." My parents must be right, we are living in sin without a commitment. You will leave me and I'll be alone, a spinster at 31. Other women will love you, no doubt, so don't linger; get on with your affairs. Just go!

Four months later, in a civil ceremony at the Provincial Governor's office in Liberia, we got married. It was all in Spanish. It sounded like a legal proceeding. Bill, resident of Tempira, age 32, profession mechanic, and Susana, neighbor of Tempira, age 31, profession mechanic (oops, slight mistake). I began laughing uncontrollably. Vows were repeated and exchanged in Spanish. There were no rings. There were no flowers. There were no kisses or smiles or hugs or good wishes. There were only two witnesses who had promised to keep this secret from everyone. OK, you're married. The first thing my new husband of five seconds did was say to the Governor as he closed his book,

"Let me see that book. What did I just commit to?"

The reluctant happiness I had half permitted myself on the way to this ceremony was shattered, as was my heart. There are no photographs from that wedding.

There were no gifts. There was no party. I had been afraid to tell anyone in Tempira that we were getting married because I had lied when we arrived and told them we already were. I couldn't let them know I had lied. It was only months later that I found out that most of the people I knew in Tempira had actually not been married until a priest came to town and did some mass ceremonies. They would have enjoyed a good party, no doubt.

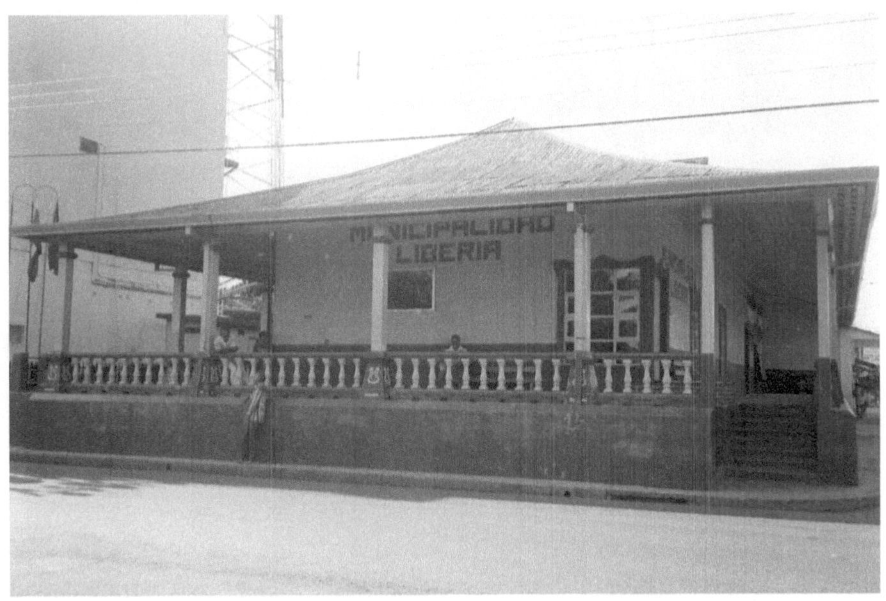

(Liberia city hall where we got married)

After the proceedings, we were invited to the "best man's" house. We had met him and his wife only 3 months earlier and were becoming friends. Before going to their house, though, we had to stop at the *Tropigas* (propane gas) store to pick up a stove his wife needed delivered. Since we had a jeep, and were right near there, it made sense, on our wedding day! to pick up the stove and take it with us. It was the least we could do, after all, she was the only one who tried to make something festive of the occasion. She had prepared her special homemade pizza. The "boys" set up the new stove then sat for hours, drinking rum until Bill fell asleep on the cement floor of their living room. It didn't look like we were going home that night. So, my friend gave me a mat to sleep on next to him and a sheet to put over me.

Happy honeymoon! This was the beginning of a marriage that should not have been!

Out of Focus

Sisterhood

Living in Guanacaste, as a neighbor with a house and husband to take care of was very different from being "*la niña Susana*" (what they called their Peace Corps volunteer), whom people sought to shelter and show only their most favorable side. As a Peace Corps volunteer in 1965 and 1966 I was invited to a barbecue at this or that *finca*, taken on *paseos* (outings) to the beach, and generally treated liked a visiting dignitary. After all, I was *their* own *Cuerpo de Paz,* a high prestige item. Once I returned in 1973, I was greeted warmly in the beginning; but since I no longer had a "mission," that of "helping people help themselves," (the Peace Corps slogan for community development), I was no longer as useful as I had once seemed. I soon learned who my real friends were. I was obviously no longer the sweet young girl who needed protection from predatory village males. I was with one. He fit right in with the men, and I could commiserate discreetly with a few select women who might not make a direct run for the nearest grapevine communications center.

Alcohol in Guanacaste is a big problem. There are usually two or three corner *cantinas* or *salones* in even the smallest villages. Commonly, the men would swig, swagger, and make promises to repent while the women would wring their hands and fret. They'd light candles or make promises to the *Virgin de los Angeles* or Saint Anthony, or they'd secretly seek magical cures from special "doctors" in Nicoya to get their men to stop drinking. Every year, someone in town is killed in a drunk driving accident, often while riding on a motorcycle. A sobbing mother in mourning weeds attends funeral mass for one of her sons, surrounded and comforted, not by her husband, but by a gaggle of other women who pat her back, blot perspiration and tears from her face, and keep her standing up in church when she feels faint from the heat and grief mixed with the suffocating smell of burning incense. The men in the back of the church look on slightly detached from the real work of yet another of life's passages. They mumble the prayers and cross themselves at the signaled moments. The voice of the hastily-summoned Spanish priest drones his insipid message to the gathered flock as though he were talking to a children's kindergarten class.

This is the ultimate act of sorority, the dreaded moment that all the hand-wringing and candle-lighting and magical cures are meant to avert. Women strike nearly immediate rapport by lamenting that a son, brother, husband, boyfriend, or father drinks too much. As a Peace Corps volunteer, I was not included; as a wife with a drinking man, I was. Seldom, if ever, would anyone mention being beaten. Yet despite all the downtrodden female faces and the apparent male domination that thrives in a society where grown men continue to behave like adolescents, the women of Guanacaste are strongly in control much of the time. They brook no nonsense, maintain few illusions, coddle their sons in lieu of cultivating partners, make do with the means they are provided and often do whatever they know best, using their own resourcefulness to bake, sew, launder, or sell home-butchered pork meat. Some bring shoes and baby clothes from Nicaragua to sell in order to have extra funds for which they do not need to thank anyone. Remember the spiders balancing on their finely spun webs?

I, too, did what I knew best to do. I taught English classes, but most people wondered aloud what I did with my time, even after I began working at the local branch of the university. They couldn't observe any "real" work, just me, often sitting in a rocking chair or at the table reading a pile of papers or typing stencils for classroom handouts then driving fifteen miles away by myself and staying away for hours at a time. They wondered, too, with slight snorts of envy, at my seeming good fortune of having a man who would go grocery shopping on his own, pick up the laundry, or wash the dishes. No sane woman should complain about such a man, even if he did drink a little too much or go with another woman every now and then. After all, those things are just ordinary male foibles, cause perhaps for resignation, not discontent or anger.

So, while many women professed friendship, most were secretly gloating that I, too, suffered pain they could recognize. To them, however, I appeared much luckier because my "problem" was such handsome *gringo* with clear blue eyes. I had been raised to trust others' opinions before my own instincts. Since no one else saw anything below normal expectations of a man, I accepted this view. I never was given to feel that my gnawing dissatisfactions were legitimate. Besides, I could hear my mother's voice in my head hammering such traditional mantras as "You've made your bed; now lie in it." Or, "learn to make the best of things; keep yourself busy." Apparently, that was how relationships were supposed to be. We need to learn to overlook others' flaws and foibles. Moreover, the Guanacastecan women all around me, young, old, and in-between, flirted constantly with Bill, sending crystalline signals more to me than to him that they would be very happy to take him off my hands, drinking problem and all.

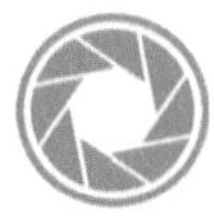

Highlights and Shadows

Danielillo

I once heard about an old-time cowhand during the days when cattle were driven on the hoof from La Cruz to Alajuela where they were slaughtered and the meat readied for export. This man is said to have had years-long relationships with eight different women, one in each of the eight towns along the route of the cattle drive. Conveniently located a day's walk from each other, these women bore numerous children over many years to this man, twelve with one, eight with another, six with a third, and so on, along the route. The count, they say, was seventy-two. It was said that he recognized them all, even if he could not call them by name. Being a poor cowhand, he could merely give them a few pennies or some pieces of candy, leaving their upbringing entirely to their respective mothers.

Other men, like Danielillo, were more responsible. A man like Danielillo, whose family owned hundreds of acres of land for cattle raising or farming, had an edge in attracting women of all social strata, whereas a "*pobre diablo*" (poor devil) doesn't have that social mobility. Men like Danielillo usually ride beautiful horses and own jeeps. They have more cash to spend buying drinks for those sycophants or friends who hover around them in the *cantinas* or at dances. They learn to be protective and possessive, willing to fight physically to defend those in their inner circle at any given moment. A woman in the company of such a man feels safe and secure; none of the slobbering drunks or young upstarts dare come near to ask her to dance or try to flirt with her. When she is with him, she is at once labeled "private property-no trespassing" even if nothing is yet going on between them. She can also expect the word soon to be out among the small-town observers who will not refrain from commenting: "Oh, was that you with Danielillo at the Rio Bar last night? Did you have a nice time?"

Men like Danielillo often have difficulties distinguishing real friends from phonies, women who sincerely care about them from those who merely see their money, land, and family status as a way to leave their own dirt-floor poverty behind. Getting pregnant may not be a conscious course of action initially, but having one of his children is a sure way to plug into the family and achieve some economic and social status, have a nicer house, maybe even have a servant rather than be one. Men like Danielillo both pursue and are pursued. Machismo is an entire social system, not merely a male characteristic.

Not unexpectedly, men like Danielillo marry at an early age. Danielillo was eighteen when he married. Adelita was a sweet but earthy and handsome girl a year younger. She lived in a small rural village on the road to the beach. Once she became "*la senora de*" (Mrs.) all the young men who had once admired her even stopped saying hello for fear of arousing Danielillo's jealousy. They became carefully respectful, even though they had known her since first grade. She quickly became Doña Adelita, reserved and matronly. A *campesina* with large hips, she was plain, rather shy, fair-skinned, a little plump, and unprepared for the Guanacastecan version of the "fast-lane" life that Danielillo led.

Danielillo was an intimidating man, with a presence larger than his real size. Even in his youth he was a hard drinker with a stubborn streak. He did not have a kind face, though there was something magnetic about him that was raw and sexual, almost hypnotic. He knew he could demand his own way either with charm or aggression, with a sneer, a shove, or merely by silently, slowly and deliberately slamming a glass or just a fist onto the table while pouring his beer. As the foam was about to overflow he might chuckle in an almost sinister way and put one of his large, calloused fingers on the rim to stem the potential cascade. He had a large scar on his left cheek from a fall he'd taken as a child. A horse had thrown him, but his foot remained in the stirrup and he was dragged a short distance, grazing his face against the barbed wire fence, until his father, Don Daniel, and one of the cowhands halted the horse. During the few moments that he dangled upside down, a loose piece of barbed wire ripped open his cheek. Nonetheless, as he grew older, that scar gave him the look of someone who might have fought hard with a machete, which he never did. Danielillo had few openly-declared enemies and fewer real friends. But he always had an eye for the ladies. His penetrating gaze and assertive grip mixed with his cowboy gallantry left little chance for rejection by those whose heart he was determined to win.

Adelita was not a common "gold-digger," like the one who snared Danielillo's younger brother Armando, according to those who know these things. Adelita never wanted to move near his parents, preferring her rural village existence with her own family, miles from the main highway. Neither was she much interested in his wheeling and cattle dealing, the legal or slightly illegal schemes Danielillo pulled off with his friends, his brothers, or others who played the same games of parlaying land and steers, losing some, winning others, and in the process scamming local distributors or middlemen. They usually remained just inside the margins of the law. Unlike some of his cohorts, he never went to jail for any of his dealings. Adelita was not a business partner, couldn't give him sound advice and just wanted to have her husband take care of her and give her lots of babies. Her lack of sophistication did not prevent her, however, from learning that Danielillo had not curbed his desire for fun with the ladies. Hearth and home-made tortillas were boring compared to the partying he had always found in the *cantinas:* the music, the booze, but most of all, being the center of attention. He missed the flirtations, the dizzying chase and the heat of winning. Giving that up in the name of marriage was not easy. In fact, he never did. A year or so after he and Adelita were married, Danielillo learned that Fini Fulano was back in Guanacaste.

Fini, which is a nickname for Josefina, was three years older than Danielillo. Her family was socially on a par with his. Her father, Don Jose and uncles owned large expanses of range land in the other direction from Danielillo's father's. Neither of their families was among the wealthiest by Guanacaste standards, though. They were too far from the bars in Liberia, the hub of real deal making along the Interamerican highway. That is where the men with patrician bellies display their silver-adorned saddles on high-stepping Arabians at fiesta time. During the rest of the year they park their Land-Rovers while they gather to drink, talk cattle, land deals, women. By comparison, the families in the *bajura* (lowlands) are minor league.

Fini's father wanted his prettiest daughter to have a cultured life, to be an educated woman, rather than a rancher's wife. Cattle ranching and farming were for her brothers. She was the first daughter to be allowed to go to the *Colegio Maria Auxiliadora*, one of the best girls' boarding high schools in San Jose. The graduation picture of her in her school uniform, a blue serge jumper with the wide, starched white collar and balloon sleeves, and a wide red satin graduation sash crossing her chest from one shoulder to her waist, used to hang next to those of her sisters, until she ran off with "that man."

Fini even got her teaching credential, which in those days only required two years of normal school. The Ministry of Education assigned her a position teaching at the school in Danielillo's town, only a mile or so from Tempira where she grew up. But Fini was not serious and "teacher-ish." She was a high-spirited, mischievous girl who made jokes and laughed easily. Her naturally husky voice and twinkling eyes made everyone around turn to listen as she spoke animatedly and passionately, giggling or poking fun irreverently at everyone. But she was also generous and kind-hearted and willing to listen to others' troubles. Fini's humor and common sense usually saw her through any crisis. Her energy attracted children and adults alike.

One day as she was riding her Vespa motor scooter back home to Tempira after school, it suddenly sputtered and lurched to a stop. A spark plug had filled with dirt from the unpaved, dusty road. Danielillo happened to be driving by in his father's Land Rover and stopped to help. He never minded dirtying his hands and certainly didn't mind doing so to help a *dama* in distress, especially the pretty, young schoolteacher. He pulled the spark plug and cleaned it off with some diesel stored in the jeep. He managed easily to prolong the job with probingly personal and flirtatious questions, wolfish grins, and soul-searching glances. When he finished, he tested the scooter out, riding up the road and back, circling around Fini closer and closer until he jerked to a stop. He invited her to have a cold drink with him. She reluctantly agreed, not wanting to appear ungrateful for his help. He suggested that they stash the Vespa and ride together in his jeep the few hundred yards to the bar near the river.

Danielillo and Fini wound up sitting there for two hours laughing and talking, drinking soft drink, his mixed with *guaro* (sugar-cane rum). He fed *pesetas* into the jukebox to hear his favorite Mexican *rancheros* and *boleros* sung by Javier Solis. During a lull in the conversation Fini looked out the side of the open bar overlooking the Tempisque River. The cattle egrets were silently gliding in formation downstream toward their nighttime perch. The setting sun cast a goldish pink tone on the white birds' undersides. A sense of calm overtook them both. The music had stopped, and no one else except the bar owner was now present. Danielillo lifted Fini's hand and held it tightly to his chest and pronounced solemnly "Someday you will be mine." She sort of giggled, but looked at his deep brown, slightly bloodshot eyes, and couldn't deny that she too felt a tugging that she knew she should resist.

In those few seconds of silence she realized she'd better go home. It would soon be dark. The late afternoon heat was abating and the mosquitoes were beginning to bite her bare ankles. The bar owner went out back to turn on the generator. Dim light broke through the clear bulbs strung amidst the beer companies' triangular advertising banners that crisscrossed the *cantina* ceiling. All three brands, Bavaria, Pilsen, Tropical, decorated the place along with cigarette company posters. Fini knew, but somehow didn't even care, that the grapevine would soon be activated by those customers who had come and gone. She knew, too, that Danielillo was married and about to become a father for the first time and that she shouldn't be feeling the strong desire to see him again.

Fini's father was more than unhappy about the attention his daughter began receiving from Danielillo. She was torn between respecting her father's wishes and her growing love and passionate attraction for Danielillo. Some say that one night he came by only to see her and she left with him; others say he actually intended to abduct her. However it happened, Fini began to live with Danielillo and became a pariah to her father and her next youngest sister, Maria Luisa, an intelligent but very self-righteous girl. Maria Luisa took it upon herself to display the family wrath against Fini, treating her like a criminal. The graduation picture was removed; she was no longer welcome in her father's house. Her mother longed to see her but was forbidden from doing so. When Don Jose was dying a few years later Maria Luisa, who, oddly enough, considers herself a good Catholic, even prohibited Fini from going to their father's bedside, either to ask for his blessing or his forgiveness, or even just to say goodbye.

Soon Fini was pregnant, and she gave Danielillo his second child. Over the next fifteen years, Adelita and Danielillo had five children, and Fini and Danielillo had four.

Adelita remained in her village. She was powerless to make him stop seeing Fini. There were no threats she could uphold. In fact, she needed him, but more, she loved him and settled for whatever bits of attention she could garner. She knew that, above all, she was his wife and that he would always come back, at least for his children.

Fini and Danielillo built a nice two-story home at the far end of Tempira, nearest the entrance to his town. He spent considerably more time with Fini than with Adelita. She helped him with his bookkeeping and other business chores. He needed her administrative skills to help him keep track of how many calves were born and when they were to be branded; how many bulls were to be castrated; which part of the herd had to be moved to which pasture area; how many steers would be trucked to slaughter next week, at what price, and so on.

For many years Fini tried hard to convince him to divorce Adelita and marry her. As much as she resented his going to see Adelita, Fini had to concede the importance of his seeing his other children. But at times, the pressures of that jealousy along with worrying constantly about whether he was drunk at two in the morning or in yet someone else's bed (because he continued to have his little flirtations, especially after Saturday night dances around the area), just got to be too much and she needed to get away. Fini bought a place in San Jose for when things weren't going well with them in Guanacaste. She would take health leaves of absence from teaching when her voice was too hoarse, or her nerves were too frazzled. She supplemented her disability checks by selling lamps one year, then encyclopedias and stainless-steel waterless cookware, the ever popular Rena-Ware. She tells a story about her first experience with a hard-selling Rena-Ware salesman who was back at the house in Guanacaste giving her an elaborate demonstration of the cookware, even jumping up and down on the back of the pot to show its durability. Danielillo had just come home from work. He grunted a greeting, looking contemptuously at the performing salesman, and went to the bedroom to lie down before dinner. Minutes later he summoned Fini and told her, "Look, pay that guy whatever he wants if you're planning to buy those pots. Just get him to stop that clown act and get him the hell out of here immediately."

Tranquility was not the hallmark of Danielillo's life either with Fini or with Adelita. He could be at once gruff and moody yet was also a gentle and proud father. He was tough yet mildly good-humored, volatile yet sometimes pathetic. He counted on Fini in ways that made it impossible for her ever to leave him, yet his drinking made life unpredictable and often unbearable. As the years passed, and he was drinking more and more, she often found it less taxing to accompany him than to stay home worrying. At times she could be seen driving the jeep with him slumped, drunk, in the passenger seat.

One night in 1978 Fini and Danielillo stopped by to pick up an extra saddle from her brother and sister-in-law who lived next door to me and Bill. It was late, perhaps 10:00 at night. Without warning Fini called out to us desperately as she banged on the flimsy wooden door. She begged for us to let her in. Something was violently wrong with Danielillo. He was in a rage, threatening her and going berserk. Her brother was trying to subdue him but he needed the help of another strong man. Bill went over, and I stayed with Fini, trying to calm her. Her face was drawn and pale and she was shaking and holding back a flood of tears with great effort. Danielillo had never behaved like this in all their years together and through all his "*borracheras*" (drunken binges). She had never felt any fear of him until now.

I don't know how or when they got him to San Jose, but the next thing I heard was that he was in the hospital, diagnosed with a rare and inoperable kind of brain tumor. That, at least, helped everyone understand his sudden and violent changes. Fini packed the children up and went to stay at her house in San Jose. Early the next day, at the hospital the doctors asked her permission to carry out some surgical procedure to relieve the pressure on his brain. But she was unable to grant the permission, facing straight on the painful fact that she was neither his wife nor a blood relative. She could not be responsible for making what might turn out to be a life or death decision and run the risk of being blamed for it later. But someone had to authorize the surgery. She decided to call Adelita in Guanacaste.

Actually she called Adelita's oldest son. He and his mother boarded the next bus to San Jose and arrived at the hospital late in the afternoon. Fini was sitting at Danielillo's side, stroking his hand. When she saw Adelita enter the room, she excused herself stoically and left, her heart breaking. Would this be the last time she would ever see Danielillo? As she exited, though, there were no unkind remarks or nasty glances. Adelita sat down in the still-warm chair Fini had just vacated. She leaned forward to put her face against his hand.

Danielillo's condition deteriorated in a matter of months. Both women visited him separately, held his hand, mopped his brow, chatted lovingly to him, pleaded with him to stay alive. One day Adelita phoned Fini. It was the first time they had ever spoken. "He's calling for you, Fini. Please come to the hospital, now."

Danielillo's funeral was held in Adelita's town where he is buried in the cemetery. He was a few months away from turning forty. Fini did not attend the funeral. She had no one except her children with whom to grieve. But a few days later she decided to go to Adelita's house. The two women were dressed in black, their eyes puffy and bare of any make-up. They greeted one another quietly, pressing each other's hand. Adelita invited Fini to sit down in the sparely furnished room. Only a few streaks of sunlight came in through the cracks in the closed shutter windows. Fini recognized one of Danielillo's white canvas cowboy hats hanging from the deer antlers on the wall near the door. It had the hand-braided horsehair hat band and tassel that Fini had once given him as a present. Adelita's middle son brought them some cold juice, and they sat sometimes in silence, sometimes tearfully.

Even eleven years later, the two women still visited occasionally; their children, half-brothers and sisters, partied and hung out together.

As one might expect, the small-town neighbors and local gossips found this to be rather peculiar.

Through the Lens

Doña Zoila's Magical Powers

Guanacaste at night looks different from anything I've ever seen. Spectacular, color-splashed sunsets are events for which one plans a trip to the beach or to an open spot in Llano Grande, (a stretch between Tempira and Liberia now an international airport). The voluminous cloud formations during the rainy season provide awe-inspiring electrical light shows, zigzagging across broad expanses of the southern night sky. And during the summer, on moonless nights, one is astounded by the enormity of the heavens and the unimaginable quantity of stars visible in that near-total darkness. Because there is hardly any ambient light coming from large cities, the sky is like a giant inverted black bowl, dotted with countless points of light. Perhaps the first riddle I learned in Spanish was about the stars:

> *¿Cuantas estrellas hay en el cielo?*
> *Cincuenta (Sin cuenta)*
>
> How many stars are there in the sky?
> Fifty. (Fifty and countless are pronounced the same.)

At that latitude a North American looking for the familiar constellations and the marker North Star must lower his sights to a mere "few inches" above the horizon. The Big and Little Dippers are nearby but sometimes hard to pick out of the crowd. It feels different to be so consciously surrounded by the universe. Infinity and the meaning of one's own life somehow intermingle. The idea of being made of the same stuff as the stars makes more sense to me in Guanacaste than anywhere else I have lived. But Guanacastecans don't seem to verbalize this, so much is it just a part of the scenery they've known forever. They aren't especially curious about the possibility of extra-terrestrial life. In fact, a common response to that sort of speculation might be "If God wanted us to believe there were life beyond the earth, He would have already told us." I do not know what Guanacastecans really feel about the exquisite beauty to which they are witness. I only know that I became aware of seeing it, the moon's phases, spiders' intricate webs, and my minuscule place in the universe by looking upward or outward.

In a place like this even outdoor plumbing has some real advantages: Showering in an outdoor stall as the sun sets allowed me to enjoy the sun-warmed water and the changing cloud swirls and streaks of pinks, purples, oranges, and deep reds that as they are cast spells over the adjacent, cactus-encircled pasture. I could look over at a charred tree that remained standing in that pasture, silhouetted against the constantly changing sky.

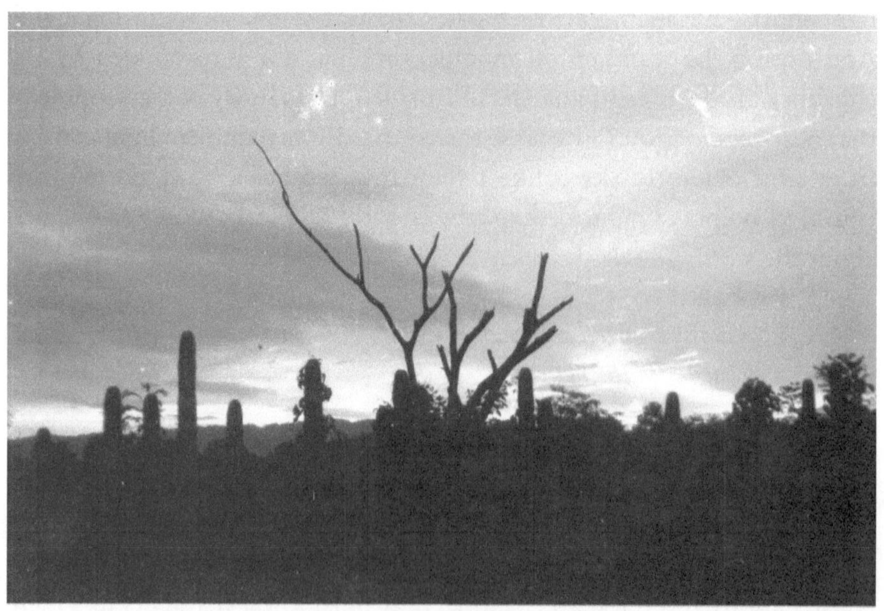

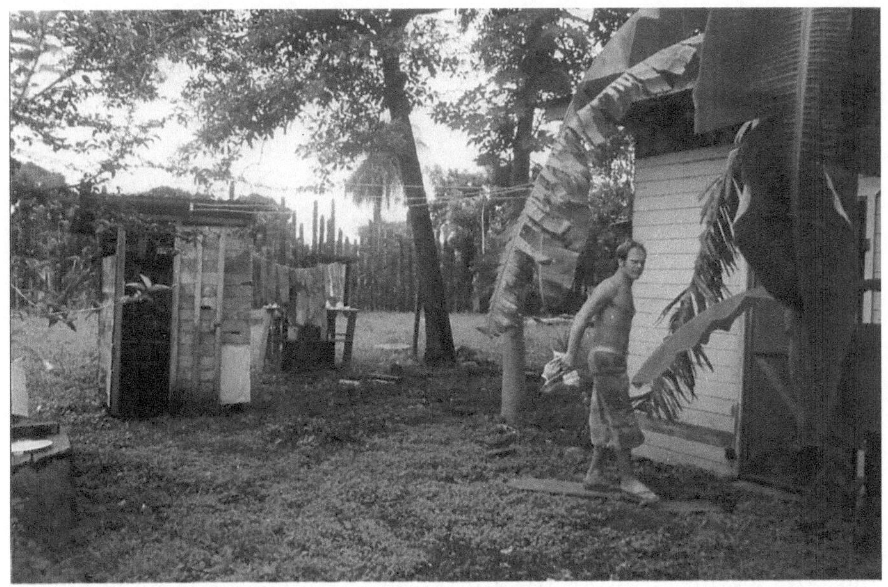

Even our pet parrots enjoyed the splashes of water and color, their beady eyes crazily dilating like a Fourth of July spinning sparkler. On my ride home late at night from class I would see large gray-white owls, perched like statues adorning the log fence posts lining the road. Suddenly and silently, one by one, they would lift their massive wings in unequaled grace, taking off into the darkness when car headlights beamed at them.

Guanacaste is full of sounds, too. Howler monkeys lounging in the trees welcome the new day well before sunrise. Scores of parrots, parakeets squawk, almost yodeling, and flutter and flap rapidly to fruit trees or sorghum fields for breakfast. Parrots fly as if it were a great effort, not with the grace of egrets or geese. Their stocky little bodies make them seem much more comfortable gnashing beaks into ripening oranges and the fleshy cashew fruit (*marañones*) for hours on end, only taking flight when startled. Other birds and insects become active at dawn, too. One can hear cows lowing, the creaking wood of an ox-cart as it lumbers on the dirt road, and today, more likely, the buzzing and zinging of small motorcycles as young men go to work at the sugar cane refinery or melon packing house.

Abruptly the sounds of bugs and birds become overlaid by those of *Radio Monumental's* 6:00 a.m. newscast, emanating from nearly every house. The rapid-fire reporting by alternating, near-monotone male voices is interrupted every few seconds by a ding-donging that indicates a new news item or advertisement. Before telephone service became readily available, the radio stations transmitted messages, long strings of messages at an appointed hour so people could tune in: 'To Lorenzo Viales in Bagaces, please meet your sister and mother arriving from San Jose this afternoon at the crossroads. Bring horses," or 'The Morales family sadly announces the death of their beloved mother and wife, Chavela. Funeral services will be held at noon in Santa Cruz, Guanacaste."

By 6:00 a.m. the day is well under way for most families. It is not uncommon for the women to rise *oscuro* (while it is still dark) at 4:30 to get the fire started for coffee and *gallo pinto* (literally, spotted rooster), the staple breakfast dish consisting of yesterday's beans and leftover rice, refried together in lard forming the purple and white mixture. The men and boys leaving for work rise a little later, customarily heading for the shower, which at that hour of the morning is cold, too cold for me to find it a pleasurable way to start the day. I was recently reminded by a friend, who had also spent many years in Guanacaste, that the water hauled from a well and not stored in a holding tank is warmer in the early morning than that in the outdoor tanks. So, using a *guacal* (gourd bowl) to dip that water was an alternative. However, showering in the early morning is something most, if not all, Guanacastecans do, partly out of a sense of cleanliness, but also because they are afraid to expose themselves to the bad *aires* (airs, drafts) that come from bathing in the late afternoon or at night. These *aires* are said surely to cause colds, stiff necks, or other maladies. It is not unusual for a Guanacastecan to warn one about the inadvisability of bathing late in the day and to attribute one's complaints of aches or a cold to having done so. (There are other times they say are also bad for bathing: after ironing clothes, baking, or immediately after coming inside from working or walking, any activity which overheats the body. It's always advisable, they say, to sit quietly for a while.)

I knew an older woman there, Doña Zoila, who said that when she was overheated she had the horrible capability of endangering an infant's life merely by looking at it. This is a variety of the *mal ojo* (evil eye), which she called the *ojo caliente* (hot eye). Guanacastecans also refer to a gadabout woman as one with a *pata caliente* (a hot foot.) While most people I knew in Guanacaste censure the late bathing because of its potential health hazard, they are frequently downright judgmental about folks who do not clean their bodies before dressing in the morning, calling them *cochino* (pig-like, dirty.) An item appeared in a 1936 issue of *El Guanacaste* called "Litanies: Guanacaste Pride" written by Fray Tempisque, a pseudonym. The fifteenth in a long list reminding Guanacastecans of their "provincial values" and modes of behavior considered special, read:

XV For your cleanliness, just fame have you conquered, genuine Guanacasteco! How you mock the *cartagos* who only bathed every eight days when you daily dip your body in the swimming holes of the rivers. . . . (Año II, No. 28, January 10, 1936).

No excuses or explanations were provided to consider the *Cartagos* mentioned living at a high elevation where the weather is much cooler than Guanacaste's arid and often oppressive heat.

Visitors sometimes come to the door without warning or apologies before six in the morning. For those who rise at 4:30 in the dark, 6:00 is no longer early. Such a visitor during our first several years back in Guanacaste was Doña Zoila.

"Suuusaaana," the quavering voice of Doña Zoila would call through the screened window from the mosaic-tiled porch. "Suuusaaaaaana," rousing me and putting me in touch with the morning already warming and abuzz with motorcycles zipping down the road and hummingbirds, bees, and swarms of other busy insects making their nectar-sucking rounds to the red hibiscus flowers outside the bedroom windows. "Suuusaaana," she called again, her broken pink plastic slippers slapping against the tile floor that just yesterday she had taken upon herself to mop for me. "*Ahi, voy, Doña Zoila, ya voy, un momentito, por favor.*" (Coming, just a minute, please.) I would leap out of bed and slip on a robe, rubbing the sleep from my eyes, embarrassed for still being in bed at 5:45 when most the rest of the world had already begun the day's chores.

Even though I was trying to live up to expectations of being a good Guanacaste wife and homemaker, I still couldn't get myself up before dawn. The challenge was greater with a partner who drank more alcohol than I ever imagined humanly possible. Instead of being loving and forgiving and compassionate, I became like many other Guanacaste wives, nagging, hand-wringing, resigned, subversively angry, a worrier. When he was away unusually late I worried, but got even angrier once he had showed up without any offering any explanation and being irritated by my concern. I grew to hate the smell of his breath, the glazed-over look, and the casual lack of concern for where he relieved himself. What was I doing mopping up piss from the bedroom floor and patching loose pieces of wall board which his fist had rammed (luckily) instead of my face? That rarely happened when he merely drank beer, so I'd begun hoping that he'd just stay away from the hard gut-rotting stuff (locally known as *guaro),* that made him an angry drunk.

Once again Doña Zoila had caught me being the lazy *gringa*! I left the man and his pillow still coming to terms with his hangover, knowing that all the men in town, with or without hangovers, were by now at work, astride their horses moving cattle or in jeeps and pickups en route to day work in the rice or corn fields. I opened the door and held out my arm to pat hers in a little embrace. I was glad to see her because she made me feel remembered, taken care of in a way, not abandoned.

A short, slightly bent woman, with no waistline, somewhere between fifty and seventy, Doña Zoila had sad, down-turned eyes and mouth, a prominent nose, and sloping shoulders around which, in the early morning she usually wore a bath towel to avoid getting a draft. Her lower jaw protruded slightly as she had no teeth to help keep her face from drooping. Her skin was the color of terra cotta and her long, drawn face was engraved with the deep wrinkles of a thousand concerns.

"*Hoooola, buenoh diiiah,* " she said, putting breaths of air where others pronounce "s," characteristic of a Guanacastecan and Nicaraguan accent. "I've got some fresh eggs here for your breakfast." She put her slightly quivering hand on my arm as she came through the door. Moving toward the kitchen table, she reached into the small brown paper sack, soft and wrinkled from multiple uses and began pulling out three eggs she'd wrapped in bits of newspaper to protect them during her walk from her place to ours. Whenever there was a shortage of eggs at the market, and before we began to keep our own chickens, I could always count on Doña Zoila to bring some eggs. I could count on her for all kinds of other things although I could never count on exactly when she would show up. I was not her only stop, either. She would stay for a little while, have a cup of coffee and some soft bread or cake. She refused my offers of anything more substantial because harder things required teeth. She'd stay for a little while but soon was off to the center of town, a block or two away.

Tempira was a town of under 1000 people, most whom were members of two or three families. The town was originally laid out around a grassy plaza, with a small church at one end and a soccer field at the other. By the late 1970s, it had expanded to include a *barrio* of outsiders who came work at the cane refinery across the river. All but a few of the houses facing the plaza were painted. It was a town with two small general stores and four *cantinas*. Sometimes Doña Zoila would find some steady day work at Yudit's, washing diapers; or at Doña Licha's scraping dried corn kernels off the cobs to be used for tortillas; or she might be trudging down the road, bringing someone a hen or rooster held closely to her side under her arm; or maybe later she'd be heading in the opposite direction carrying two corked liquor bottles now filled with fresh milk.

"Why Doña Zoila, how did you know 1 needed some eggs today?" Her toothless mouth would open in a broad smile and she would howl her characteristic, hoarse cackle and tell me that she has had strong intuitive powers since she was a little girl in Matagalpa, Nicaragua. It was these and other powers that her mother had been told would disappear should she be forced to learn to read. (I once had offered to teach her to read, but she said it would be harmful "*me hace daño,*" and patted the back of her neck.)

She also knew that Bill drank too much. One morning she told me that he needed to be very careful of his health. She fished into the pocket of her loose-fitting pink, yellow, and black flowered dress, and her wrinkled hand came up with a small bundle, a man's handkerchief knotted and tied with a string. Her knobby fingers patiently worked to undo the knots. I watched with anticipation, unable to guess what magical curiosity she would show me. When she got it opened, among the coins and scraps of paper, one of them a lottery ticket, she selected a small, tube of cloth loosely sewn together to hold in the hidden contents.

'This," she said, "is for Don Bill to wear pinned inside his shirt pocket over his heart. It will protect him." She really liked him and thought of his drinking as some sort of possession by an evil demon that could be held at bay with such protective charms.

"What is it?" I asked, regarding the bulky little packet she herself had obviously fashioned of flowered cloth. I was sitting beside her at the table, having forgotten even to put some water on for coffee. She knew how I couldn't stand his drinking to such excess, and she knew, too, that it wasn't right for a strong, strapping, young man not to be outside working early in the morning.

'These are *siete frijoles* (seven beans). I am going to look for some leaves later, but this bundle you must pin inside his shirt pocket. He should wear it always." Having read many of the then-popular Carlos Castaneda's Don Juan books, and finding the *I Ching* (Chinese Book of Changes) to be meaningful, as well as generally feeling that spiritual and healing powers are special gifts to be respected and appreciated, I always welcomed Doña Zoila's interventions. It made me feel safe and warm that she was trying to take care of us. If wanting to believe in magical cures is part of what makes them work, I wanted to believe more than anything that she really could exercise some power. Her good intentions alone helped me, even if they did not affect anyone else.

When I first mentioned her to some of my neighbors, they scoffed at her *remedios,* calling her an ignorant old Nica, and laughing at me for believing her *babosadas* (foolishness). They said they expected more from me, someone with my *preparacion* (schooling). So I simply stopped telling them about her. I used to receive frequent little sarcastic jabs though, "So, how's your good friend Doña Zoila?" or "*Mire,* (Look) Susana, there goes Doña Zoila. Maybe she's looking for you." People dismissed her on the one hand, but on the other would utilize her services and pay her a pittance for her trouble. She once grumbled to me that this one well-off family was the worst. She'd spent a whole day scraping the dried kernels off corn cobs which are used for making *tortillas.* It's a time-consuming job that is especially hard on the hands. After she'd filled two five-gallon lard cans, they'd given her only two *colones*, about 25¢ and barely enough in those days to buy a quart of milk. But there were tasks she would refuse to do. Although she would wash soiled diapers, she would not change a baby or even lift it up. I thought it was because of her trembling hands and inability to fasten a safety pin securely. But she was afraid, she told me, that she would harm the baby since she had an "*ojo caliente.*" This was another of her powers, but one that she greatly feared. Most, if not all, babies in Guanacaste, when they are taken outdoors are wrapped in little blankets or a towel and have their faces covered. There are some health reasons for this custom, such as to keep little flying insects from getting in their eyes and mouth. Many mothers try to protect them from the sun's unrelenting and intense rays because they don't want the baby's skin to turn dark. But a reason that most will not readily admit to is that they want to protect the baby from "*mal ojo*" (evil eye) a harmful spell cast intentionally, out of jealousy, revenge, or simple malice. But Doña Zoila was talking about something different. I had never heard any other such references to *ojo caliente*, and no one ever told me that Doña Zoila had ever hurt any babies. Why she believed she was capable of such harm is something she never told me.

Once when we were getting ready to leave for a few days, Doña Zoila decided to bring some things to protect our house while we were away. She had an old perfume bottle with a puff of brownish fuzzy material stuffed inside it. She said it was a "*nido de macuá*," the nest of a small bird, I think. She instructed me very solemnly to get a bottle of "*siete perjumes*" (seven perfumes) to pour in the bottle with the nest. (I never did get the perfume, but the little nest stayed for years on a ledge over the door from kitchen to the living room.) In addition, she said we needed to put four lemons around the outside of the house, one at each corner and that would protect the house from harm. She also recommended that her brother Roque stay as a watchman (*cuidador*). He could feed the parakeets and water the garden every afternoon. That worked out quite well. Before we left, I asked if she needed or wanted anything from San Jose. Without hesitation Doña Zoila requested that we bring her a new blanket. Bill took charge of the errand and stopped at all the stalls in the central market until he found just the right one. After that she always told us what she wanted us to bring her when we were heading to the city. Some people thought she was pretty bold to expect us just to bring her things without her making any indication to offer to pay; others thought she was beginning to take advantage of us. I tried to bring her what she requested. Sometimes it was beyond my means, but I never really wanted to think that she was trying to take advantage. After all, she was never stingy with her advice or stories. Everything else was based on financial transactions characteristic of the most businesslike exchanges: eggs or chickens for sale; dropping in unexpectedly to wash some clothes or dishes when she needed some cash, and so on.

One day a North American friend who lived a few kilometers away arrived. She got off the lumbering yellow school bus aptly named "*El Consentido.*" (the Spoiled One). Most local transport in Guanacaste consisted of these retired school buses, now brightly painted, often brought from a Mid-western school district in the U.S. *El Consentido* made several trips each day back and forth from Sardinal to Liberia. Timing a visit correctly, a friend could arrive around eleven and go home on the return trip around two. That day as my friend stepped out of the bus, a wasp stung her hand, which instantly puffed up in allergic reaction. Luckily, Doña Zoila was there when my friend came into the house clutching her swelling hand. Doña Zoila mentioned something about some leaves and immediately left, leaving us both wondering what she was up to.

About ten minutes later she brought some dark green *raspa* leaves (usually used for scrubbing pots because of their abrasive surface) and proceeded to lay them on my friend's swollen and, by now, throbbing hand. Within a minute, the pain subsided and the allergic reaction began to dissipate.

On another occasion, Doña Zoila brought an armful of leaves wrapped in newspaper" two different kinds: *guarumo* and *junquillo* that she had gathered to boil up in a large pot. From the dark infusion she made compresses with old towels for my knees that were stiff with pain. I would sit with my legs extended, supported on another chair, for an hour or so, while she changed the towels, reheating the tea-like liquid.

As I sat there Doña Zoila would tell me about her life: the reasons she had left her abusive husband years before or about some indignity she had suffered at one of the more well-to-do households in town, or about Nicaragua. We repeated this procedure over a number of weeks. I heard fantastic stories, most of which I have forgotten, that used to give me goose bumps despite the hot towels on my legs. One story I remember was about

> "A man in a Nicaraguan village who was so poor that he could not support his large family. One day he went to the church and knelt to pray at the statue of the Jesus, a beautiful statue, the pride of the village because this statue had gold sandals. Everyone used to rub or kiss the feet of the statue in hopes that the Lord would

> grant their supplication. The feet were rubbed smooth. This man prayed very hard, telling the statue how poor he was and how hungry his children were, and lo and behold, the Lord gave the man one of his golden sandals. Of course, when it was discovered that the man had the gold sandal everyone thought he had stolen it from the statue, and they were very angry with him. But to prove his innocence, the man told the townspeople to go back to the church with him and let the Lord vouch for his innocence. They all went back and the man prayed again at the foot of the statue that now only wore one gold sandal. He begged the Lord to prove his innocence to the people and so the Lord gave him the other sandal."

"And this really happened?" I would ask, not wanting to seem too skeptical. I thought I had missed something or hadn't understood because sometimes I would lose track of who was doing what as in Spanish it's not as necessary to use pronouns as it is in English.

'This really happened," she would say solemnly, "um hmmm." She looked completely earnest, and you could tell she herself believed what she was telling me.

My rational, college-educated side wanted to say, "Yeah, sure." But at the same time the little hairs on my arm would stand up and tears would well up in my eyes as she told her stories. I accepted her at her word and wanted to know more, what happened next, and what became of the man. I knew that she was telling me things that many people believe but few would have ever told me, perhaps fearing I would think them ignorant or gullible.

"Oh, so many things have happened," she would say. I could only wonder what was hidden behind her strong, sad, Indian face. Her stories were timeless. They might have been things she experienced just yesterday or years before, or they could be stories heard from other people but told as if she had direct involvement. Or maybe they were stories she invented on the spot from things she saw in her head. It really didn't matter.

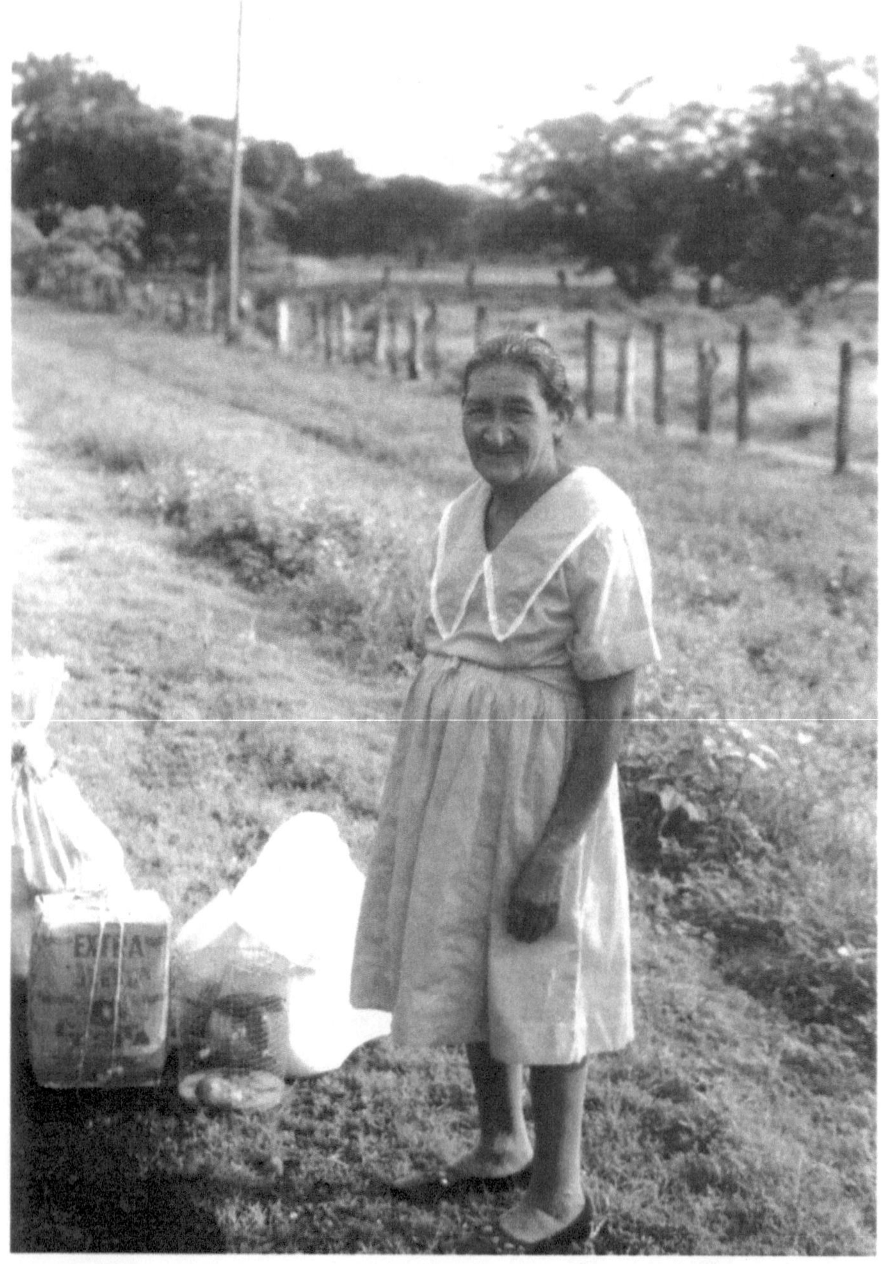
EXTRA

One morning around 9:30 I saw Dona Zoila standing on the gravel shoulder of the road fifty or so feet up from our house. She was wearing a clean, pressed cotton dress and at her feet were several carton boxes and rice sacks tied with cord along with a bird cage with a little parrot, and the suitcase we'd once brought her from San Jose. Her gray-streaked hair was still wet from the shower and pulled back in two loosely tied, unbraided sections away from her deeply-etched sun-leathered face. She was wearing new pink woven plastic shoes and was waiting for the ten o'clock "*pulman*" bus to take her to San Jose.

"Where are you going? And when are you coming back?" I couldn't help but be surprised at this abrupt departure.

"I'm going to Limon to be with my daughter, the one who works as a cook for the banana finca over near Sarapiqui. *Quien sabe*? (who knows) when I'll be back. Only God knows that."

The giant blue Mercedes bus appeared in the distance, making several stops along the way before reaching us. Together we flagged it down. The *cobrador* (helper who collects the fare) jumped out of the bus and opened the luggage compartment, tossed in her bags, let the hydraulic hatch door whoosh closed and turned the handle to relock the compartment. Then he gave Doña Zoila a hand as she hoisted her bent, bulky body into the bus. She had said she'd be back, but tears came to my eyes as if I were saying goodbye to her for the last time. I worried about her. What if she got sick and couldn't get medical help in that remote banana-growing district? What if she were bitten by a snake as she made her rounds over there? What if her daughter needed her for a long time? I realized how I would miss her and how much I'd come to depend on her daily visits and her doting attention. And the magic of her stories.

Weeks, usually months would pass. I would ask Nicomedes, her nephew who was the local telegraph operator, or old Santiago who was married to her sister Consuelo, about her. No one had heard a word from her. Sometimes I'd get a letter or an old Christmas card (even in July) postmarked Limon written by her daughter telling me that Doña Zoila was well and sent her greetings to me and Bill. Then without warning, maybe months later, I'd hear the familiar footsteps at 6:00 in the morning and her voice calling Susaaaannna.

On one occasion she left, however, and I never saw her again.

Close-Up

Don Goyo, Noble Cowboy

Las Espuelas, El Bramadero, Los Boyeros, La Ronda are names of big shots' hangouts, restaurants and hotels in Liberia whose clients drive Toyota jeeps and Range Rovers. Those names, which translate as the spurs, the tethering post, the ox-cart drivers, and pasture border, all relate to some aspect of Guanacaste's image as Costa Rica's cowboy and cattle country. It is rare to see a horse hitched outside any of these places, however. The much-romanticized Guanacaste *sabanero* and his faithful steed now are cast in concrete perched on a cement pedestal at the entrance to town. The statue sits steadfastly between the Rotary Club's geared wheel and another revered icon, the statue of a large woman cradling a child, as though she were the Guanacaste *pietá*. The statue of the *sabanero* with his tilted hat and rolled lasso is a larger-than-life testimony to earlier times when most Guanacaste men were either cowboys, machete swingers, or big shots. It wasn't until things began to change in the 1970s that some of the community members found it necessary to remind everyone of a disappearing past. They took a notion to erect statues and give awards on Guanacaste Annexation Day, July 25, to honor those old-timers who, just by living and working, had forged the legendary image that today is practically a logo, so self-conscious has it become. It is rare, but not impossible, to see anyone who is as noble, courageous, and dignified as the one cast in bland, gray concrete.

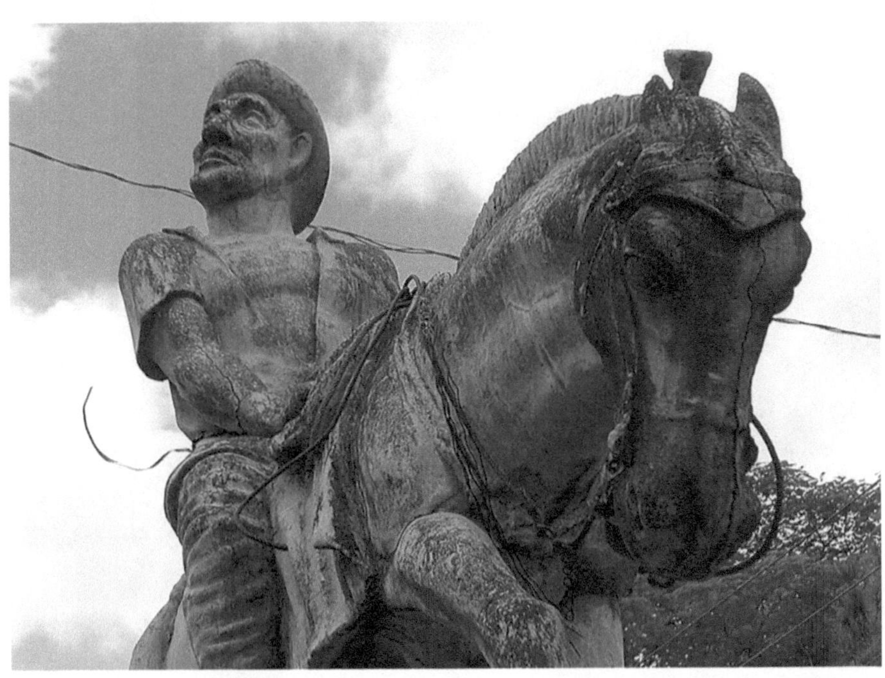

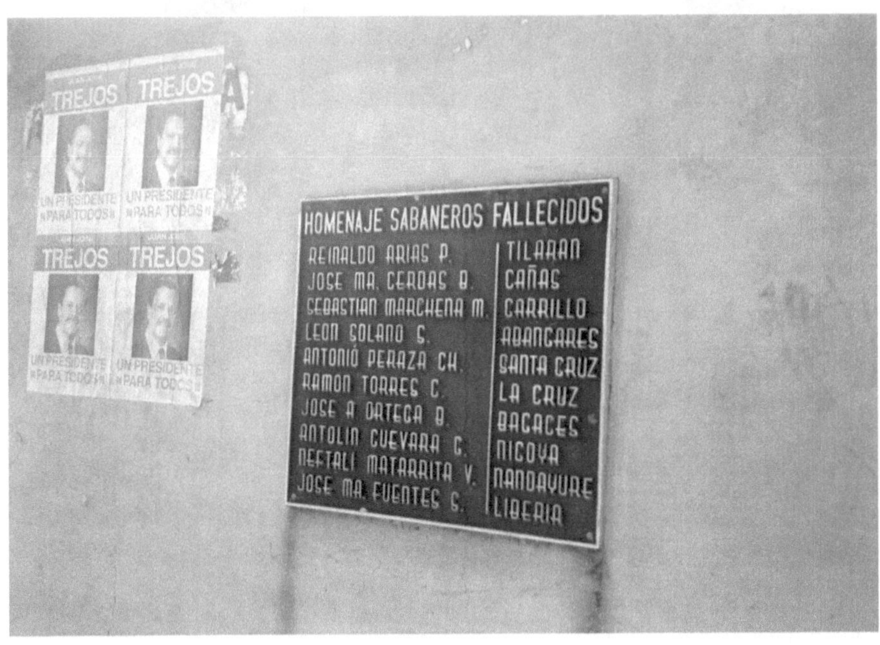
TREJOS
UN PRESIDENTE PARA TODOS
TREJOS
UN PRESIDENTE PARA TODOS
TREJOS
UN PRESIDENTE PARA TODOS
TREJOS
UN PRESIDENTE PARA TODOS
HOMENAJE SABANEROS FALLECIDOS
REINALDO ARIAS P. | TILARAN
JOSE MA. CERDAS B. | CAÑAS
SEBASTIAN MARCHENA M. | CARRILLO
LEON SOLANO S. | ABANGARES
ANTONIO PERAZA CH. | SANTA CRUZ
RAMON TORRES C. | LA CRUZ
JOSE A ORTEGA B. | BAGACES
ANTOLIN GUEVARA G. | NICOYA
NEFTALI MATARRITA V. | NANDAYURE
JOSE MA. FUENTES S. | LIBERIA

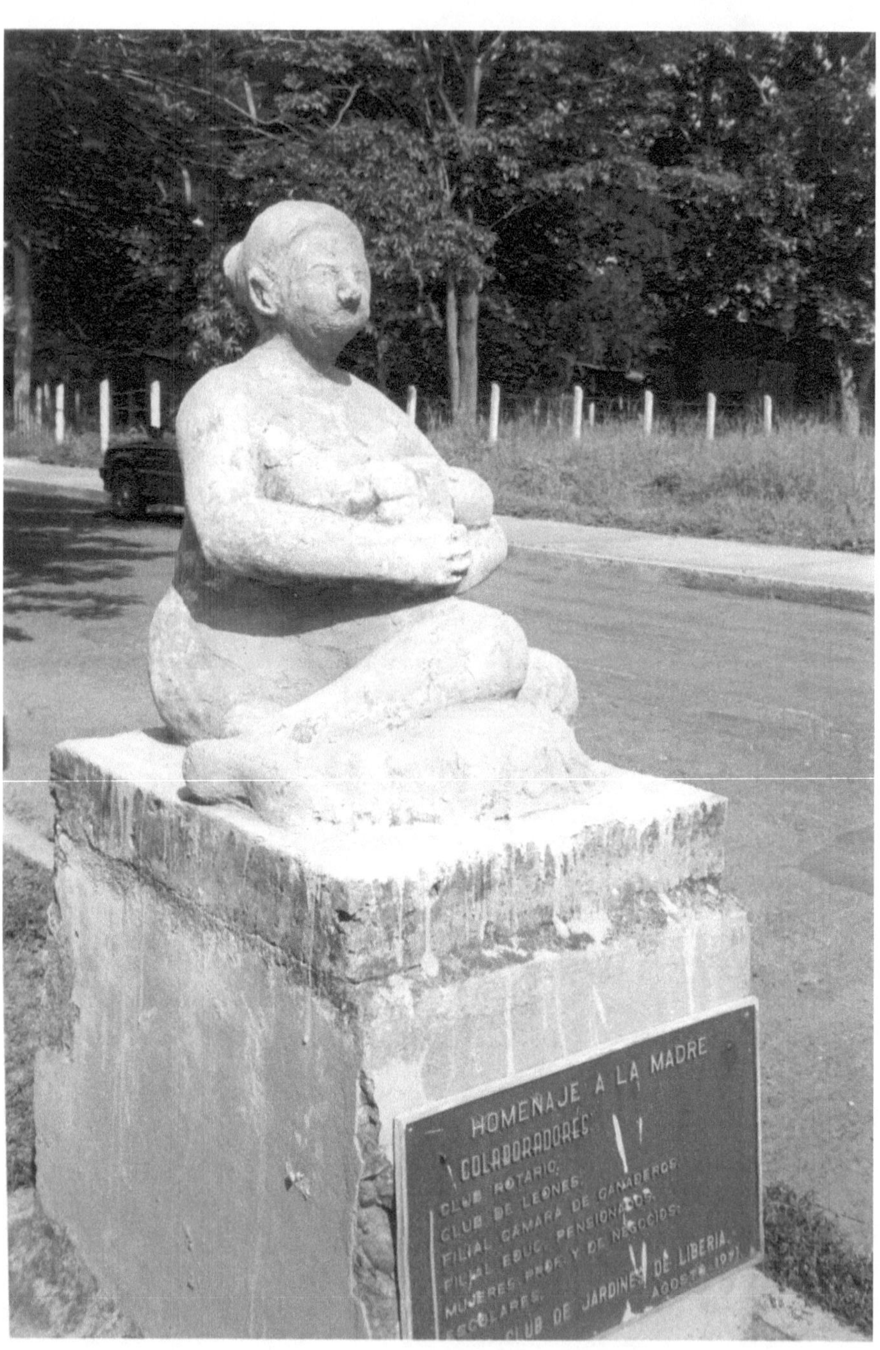
HOMENAJE A LA MADRE
COLABORADORES:
CLUB ROTARIO;
CLUB DE LEONES.
FILIAL CAMARA DE GANADEROS.
FILIAL EDUC. PENSIONADOS.
MUJERES PROF. Y DE NEGOCIOS.
ESCOLARES.
CLUB DE JARDINES DE LIBERIA.
AGOSTO 1971

One such hero cowboy befriended us. Slight and wiry, severely bowlegged and with the most knotted arthritic hands I'd ever seen, Don Goyo, or Goyito, a nickname for Gregorio, was of that older generation of cowboys, one of the few with a wealth of knowledge about horses, from how to train them to how to cure them.

From riding the area since he was a small boy, Don Goyo had developed an extraordinary ability to know where he was anywhere in the middle of the wilderness. He was so familiar with every inch of terrain, angles of light, and the stars that he couldn't get lost. He could identify every kind of tree just by looking at a stick and knew which different woods were good for what purposes, for fences, houses, bottle stoppers, rice threshers, or tethering posts. He knew the winds: what direction meant dry or rainy weather, how much time there would be until the showers began by reading the cloud formations or the circling patterns of a lone hawk. He could speculate quite accurately from the signs whether the entire corn-growing season would be favorable or not. By the phases of the moon he knew when it was time to plant which staple crops: *la luna menguante* (a waning moon) for *yuca* or other tubers and roots which needed to develop beneath the surface, or a *luna creciente* (waxing moon) for corn and other above-the-surface crops which needed the upward pull to grow strong and tall. He knew all the native poisonous and non-poisonous snakes and bats; and where their caves were hidden. He could find baby parrots inside large, brown termite nests built on ash tree limbs.

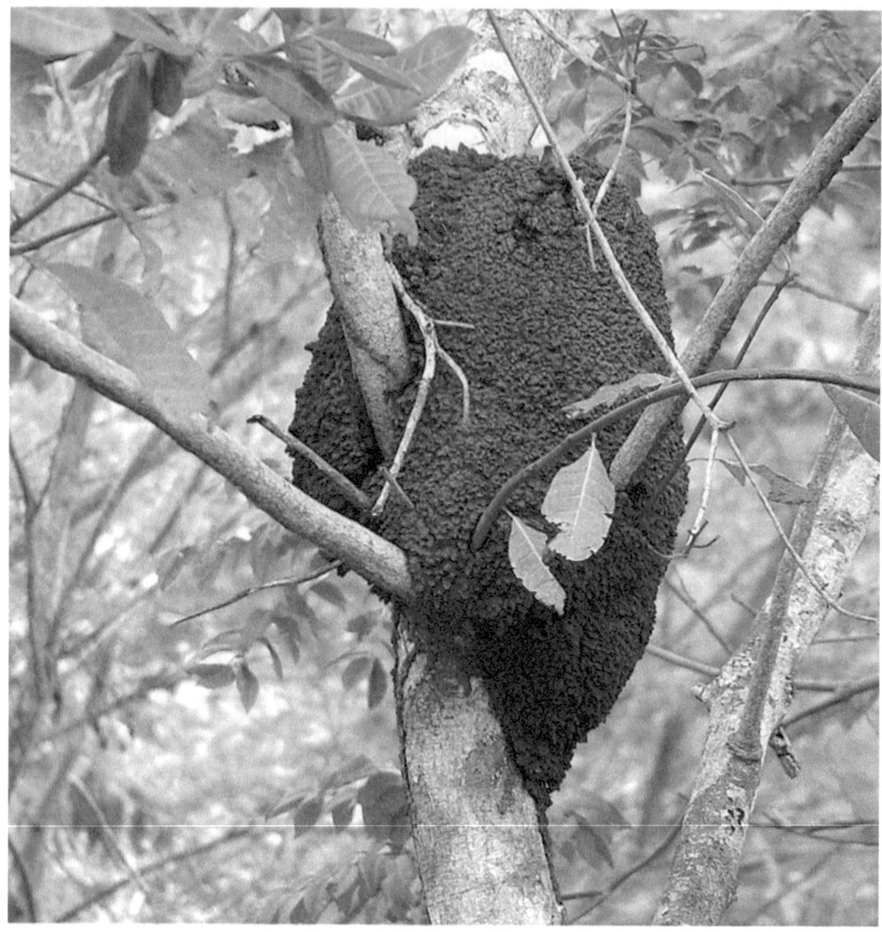

He knew where mountain lions, *jaguars* and wild peccary hogs, *sahinos* lived in the distant hills and where they sometimes came down for water or prey. He knew where a dead cow or horse lay by the *zopilotes* (a kind of vulture) flocking to dine on the rotting flesh. Goyo knew the soils, too: where to avoid leading a horse because the soil was like quicksand and where to locate an underground spring, *ojo de agua,* hidden in the recesses of arid hillsides. He knew the shortcuts and the safest routes for moving cattle from the beach to the ranches along the Tempisque River. And he knew the deepest, fastest-moving spots in the river to avoid and those where the *lagartos* (alligators), patrolled the river banks just beneath the surface, waiting for a lone calf or unaware dog. They say that the small son of one of the cooks at San Jacinto was playing near the edge of the river while his mother was washing clothes, and an alligator snatched him away before anyone even knew it. Goyo knew about *El Cadejos*, the legendary black dog that safeguards men, especially drunks, and *La Cegua*, the dangerous lady in white who asks male passersby, often drunk, to give her a lift and after they become attracted to her, she turns out to have the face of a skeleton or a horse. He knew about *La Llorona*, the weeping woman of legend, who is said to have abandoned her children at the river, some say even drowning them, whose wails can occasionally be heard at night by men riding or walking along the river as she searches fruitlessly for her children. And Goyo could also recognize the tracks of the *duendes*, the little gnomes who wear red suits and walk backwards and come out usually around *Semana Santa* (Holy Week). He remembers the time when a lady who lived near the woods had to tie her small boy to the leg of his sleeping cot to keep him from following the *duendes* into the forest. And he also knew about *La Mona,* the woman who seduces a man at night and turns up at his house the next day asking his wife for salt and then hangs out in a nearby tree as a hairy monkey. That one is hearsay, though, because Goyo doesn't have a wife. He lives with his two sisters and their children. Other things he knew about included how to secure knots to haul trees so that the weight was properly distributed and didn't strain the horse. The knife he always carried had an edge that was so sharply honed that he could effortlessly slice a one-inch *manila* (jute rope) with one hand, holding the end of the rope in his mouth. He could determine certain things about a horse's health by the color of its eyes, by its teeth and gums, by the curve in its spine, and by the texture of its hooves. Even Don Alberto, who was one of the best-known horsemen in Guanacaste, would tip his hat to old Goyo and send for him to get a "second opinion" when necessary. Goyo was also a fearless cowboy.

I don't remember how Don Goyo came to be Bill's friend. It must have been when Bill was buying a horse from Danielillo and Don Alberto suggested he ask for Goyo's opinion about the animal's health. The horse had been bitten by a vampire bat some years earlier and still had a lump on its neck as a result. Otherwise it was a beautiful horse, a handsome roan gelding named *El Colorado,* good for work, at a decent price, and with an impressive gait, a horse definitely for an experienced rider. Goyo thought the bat wound was well-enough healed that it shouldn't be a problem. Sometimes, he explained, a wound is poorly healed and becomes like a beacon, attracting bats again and again to the same spot, so that over time, the animal becomes weaker and weaker from having his blood sucked by the *vampiros* and eventually it dies. The saliva of the bat contains an anesthetizing substance so an animal, or sleeping human for that matter, would not feel the bat's presence.

Don Goyo went with Bill to Liberia to help him buy the saddle and other gear for *El Colorado* from an old saddlemaker who Goyo knew would give him a fair price, not one specially inflated for the *gringo.* They bought a well-constructed bridle with a small stainless-steel bit that wouldn't mistreat the horse's mouth; a foam pad to cushion the *albarda,* comfortable stirrups with hand-tooled leather casings; and a good *manila* that would be tied to the *albarda* for lassoing cattle or another horse. Goyo supervised Bill's dressing the horse the first few times, and together they rode out to a piece of land Bill had bought to use as pasture land. Goyo pointed out quirks and strengths he observed in *El Colorado*, helped soften and break in the *manila* by unrolling and bending it a bunch, and taught him how to keep the gear and the horse clean. It had been a while since he, himself, had had new gear and a new horse of his own, so Goyo seemed to be enjoying teaching Bill about what went where and how to do things efficiently.

"No, Don Bill, not like that, *asi. como lo hago yo*" (like this, the way I'm doing it).

One day he came to the house with a cow horn fashioned to carry *carbolina* for cleaning the ticks off the horse. He had carved a smoothly fitting base from a piece of *cortez* wood that left no cracks or crevices around the rim and a little plug for a top, which also fit snugly. It seemed amazing that Goyo could use his tightly twisted hands so skillfully to create such a finely crafted item or to tie a bowline and any variety of other complicated knots. He never mentioned feeling pain, though his hands with such curled fingers and bent wrists looked uncomfortable. Goyo, for that matter, looked more at ease on top of a horse than walking on the ground. At 125 pounds, his small stature and bowed legs did not exactly give him a "he-man" look. And standing next to six-foot, muscular Bill,

Goyo looked like the proverbial "ninety pound weakling." That, of course, was a mistaken perception.

One morning, very early, around 4:30 or 5:00, not quite dawn, Bill left with Goyo and Tacho, our next door neighbor to move some fifteen or twenty young, *novillos* (uncastrated bulls) to the pasture the Tacho was renting near Playa Panama, about ten miles away. They figured the whole task should be accomplished in a few hours, maybe by lunch time, or a little after. When he left, Bill said that later in the afternoon he'd be able to go to town with me to buy groceries and maybe we'd stay to eat dinner at *Cuatro Mares*, my favorite Chinese restaurant, and take in a movie, like some old Charles Bronson shoot-em-up. Lunchtime came and went, and by mid-afternoon I began anticipating their imminent arrival.

Night falls early in Guanacaste. It's usually dark by 5:00 or 5:45 all year round because Costa Rica is only ten or twelve degrees above the equator. By that time I was beginning to go into worry mode. Had something happened? Why weren't they back yet? This was before the age of cell phones! I thought of going out in the car to look for them but really had no idea where to begin. Besides, I had become something of a laughing stock because previously I had gone out to search for Bill in the *cantinas* even twenty miles away. I was afraid something awful had happened since he often drove his motorcycle after drinking heavily. One time he had fallen and was sleeping on the shoulder of the road when I found him.

Sometimes the embarrassment of finding him was worse than the pain of not knowing where he was. Guanacastecan wives do not do such things. It was clearly considered odd gringa behavior to go out looking for your man. But because they had known me for so many years, people also felt a little sorry for me for thinking I could actually influence fate.

Of course, my feelings or fears never discouraged the men from inviting Bill to a beer, nor did the thought of my worrying ever give him pause about accepting their invitations for that beer. Actually, in Guanacaste, there is no such thing as *one* beer. The person who invites you to a beer, pays. *Cantina* etiquette, if it can be called that, requires that you return the invitation. After that, each successive beer may be called *el zarpe* (the last one, the one for the road, from the word *zarpar*, to set sail. I wonder if setting sail requires that one be "three sheets to the wind"!). That first ice cold beer, *bien fria* after hours of hard work in the hot sun, may quench the thirst but more often is merely the prelude to some serious drinking. It might be "chased" by a shot of *guaro* (a crudely distilled sugar cane rum). *Cantineros* keep their customers ordering more drinks by providing free rounds of delicious snacks, *bocas* ranging from illegally-obtained turtle eggs to marinated fish cocktail (*ceviche*), tripe stew (*mondongo*) to tasty pieces of stewed chicken in seasoned tomato sauce. (*Gringos* often recommend *cantinas* to each other by the kind and quantity of *bocas* they serve, certainly a far cry from the peanuts and pretzels usually served in most U.S. bars. If you're not much into drinking but are stuck in a *cantina* with people who are, at least it's possible to fill up on the *bocas* as each round of beer or *guaro* brings more little plates of snacks.)

Sitting in a bar nursing a bottle of grape Fanta or a fresh fruit *refresco* while Bill drank himself "mellow", usually with some other men, was never my idea of a good time. Apparently, after the first year or two, it lost some of its charm for Bill, too, he said. At first it served as his classroom for language lessons. After nine months he was as fluent, though much of his vocabulary were words I had never even heard, let alone used, in those two years that I had lived there as the well-sheltered Peace Corps volunteer. He said the conversations only seemed to have three topics: work, women, and sex, usually teasing about someone else's "hydraulics," or what foods are good to make it work better. According to Bill, these conversations were like what he remembered from high school locker rooms. So when he began to get bored by the same conversations and stale jokes that he soon understood but never found funny or was too drunk even to understand at all, he learned to have a few drinks with whoever was inviting him and then buy as many beers as he could stuff into his jute saddle bags or button inside his shirt. Or he'd buy a liter of rum instead. Then he'd come home and proceed to finish off those bottles, smoke some pot, play some guitar that sounded like Stephen Stills or Bob Dylan, and if the *cantinas* were still opened, he might make a run for some more, against my cajoling, pleading, resentfulness, or just plain nagging.

Knowing his style, I found it odd that Bill would be spending so much time in a *cantina* that day with Goyo and Tacho. I later learned what happened that day. After they'd left the *novillos* at the pasture, the three realized how thirsty they were, out there in the blisteringly hot mid-morning sun. So they decided to stop at the rustic, bamboo and thatch *cantina* that sits only a few meters from where high tide laps at the sandy white beach near Playa Panama. Local fishermen and their sons unload their catch of the day there and lay nets out to dry. Some female tourists in skimpy bathing suits wander down the beach looking for just the right spot to lay down their towels and purses. The men's attention is at first riveted by so much white flesh flashing before their eyes, but they know it's out of their range and return to their tasks at hand. The scene is picture-postcard idyllic for tourists, but, like many familiar things, even the blue sky and calm sea turn ordinary after a while. It is nothing out of the ordinary for men, when their work was complete, for someone to suggest stopping for a beer and a bite to eat before going home for lunch, a shower, and a nap. After the first three beers, Bill and Tacho settled in to the customary camaraderie of ordering more and more beer. The empty bottles, filling up with cigarette butts, on the small turquoise-colored table took up more and more space. After a few hours Tacho left.

Don Goyo knew Bill's capacity, and he could have left him there, too. Dusk was falling, and Bill had dozed off while fellow drinkers came and went. The tide, which had been high when they arrived, then was low, was starting to come in again. The clatter of shells and pebbles with each incoming wave was hypnotic. Goyo, like one of those loyal sidekicks in old cowboy movies, chose to stay with him, to help him get home because he knew by then that Bill wouldn't be able to negotiate the spirited gelding in the dark, through the woods. And the horse wouldn't know any other route except the way he had traveled in the morning. It was too dark a route for someone who didn't know the land.

Meanwhile, back at home, I was getting increasingly concerned. When it appeared that the planned trip to shop, eat Chinese food, and see the Bronson movie was not going to materialize, I fixed something for dinner, went over to the neighbor's to see if her husband had come home or if they knew what was delaying Bill (as if by then I couldn't guess!). I visited for a while then went back to the house, and tried to read. But I couldn't concentrate and besides, the single yellow bug light in the ceiling socket was too dim to read by, and my eyes started to droop. The sheer curtains I'd made two years before were billowing slightly in the evening breeze. I stepped out onto the tiled porch and looked both ways up the highway to see if I could detect either sound or movement. The clear silver crescent moon was low in the sky, yet its light cast shadows on the bowed asphalt road. A few men were leaving Dona Mencha's bar a hundred yards up the street, as one car engine started and a Landrover jeep drove off in the opposite direction. Otherwise there was no one in sight. The neighbor's lights had already gone out for the night. I decided that except for worrying and waiting, there was nothing I could do. I went to bed around 8:30 and took a long while to doze off.

Around 10:30, the dog began barking and even the parakeets were stirring and murmuring in their cage. I heard the angry voices of men shouting amid the clopping and skidding sound of horses on the gravel. They were struggling to a halt inside the gate. "Don Bill, *ehhhyaaa*! Don Bill, *apiese*, get down, Don Bill, *APIESE*! I ran out, and there was Bill, leaning precariously, slumping out of his saddle which was also easing to one side, and practically sliding on top of Don Goyo. His one arm and shoulder were partially draped around his horse's shiny wet neck, lassoed tightly close to Don Goyo's horse.

Horses are not used to being quite that close, and these two were bobbing their heads in discomfort and pawing and stomping in rebellious gestures. Goyo was barely visible with the mountain of Bill's weight on him. Bill's shirt was in tatters, his back was scratched and bleeding, and he was drunk enough no longer to be friendly and polite to Don Goyo, just plain angry, as though he too were being reined in against his will. Goyo also sounded angry, exasperated and very stern. He had seen too much in his days to consider this so out of the ordinary, but he was most pained, he told me later, to see the rider so uncaring about his horse.

Don Goyo recounted the journey from the beach, how Bill had fallen asleep right there in the *cantina*, but after a few hours abruptly awakened and in his stupor decided there and then it was time to leave and go home to lie down. He jumped on *El Colorado* and took off in a hard gallop. Goyo realized instantly that this could turn tragic, and without hesitation mounted his own horse and took off after Bill. He caught up with him, lassoing *El Colorado* to a slow walk. But Bill kept losing his balance, and several times he fell off the horse. Goyo had to help him re-mount. Each time he thought Bill would be under control, he'd loosen the rope, but Bill would take off, and the chase was on again. On a few occasions dry, low-hanging tree branches glanced off Bill's head and scraped along his back. On one fall, he slid against the rough bark of a tree that abraded his skin; beneath the remaining shirt shreds his back was streaked with thin, blood-oozing lines and blotches that looked rasped by a carrot shredder. Goyo stayed with him for ten miles of this madness, and by the time they arrived home, he was shouting stern reprimands, as though dealing with a belligerent child. "Get down, Don Bill! Get down and stand up like a man!"

When we got him seated on a kitchen chair, together Goyo and I removed Bill's shirt, and I tried to wash down the bloody and by now scabbing scratches. He wouldn't sit still and brushed us both away with a swipe of his arm as he stood up, steadying himself for a few seconds against the table. He stumbled towards the spare room where a large cot was set up. After first missing the entrance to the bathroom, he released his urgent bladder against the living room wall. I was mortified that Don Goyo should witness this, and I was angry that Bill showed so little respect for his home. When he got to the cot he called out for me to bring him a large jug of water to keep by his bedside. My feelings of rage, sadness, and frustration were drowned by the need to take care of him. What thirst of my own was being quenched by his alcoholism? What combination of "good-wife expectations learned from my mother's and Guanacaste's women was I accepting as more legitimate than my own feeling that this just wasn't right?

Goyo and I then dealt with the sweaty, snorting horse. Goyo removed all the gear but the bridle on his head, and I gave him a bucket of water to drink while Goyo hosed the poor beast down and together we slicked the cool water off his back.

"Doña Susana, you should have seen him; it was terrible. He would take off and run this poor beast so fast. If I hadn't have stayed with him, *quien sabe* (who knows) what would have happened?"

I think we both knew what might have happened. Goyo helped me drag the *albarda* and other gear to hang in the tack room. He had a glass of water, and limped through the door. Thanking him and trying to hold back tears, I closed the gate after him and watched as he, back atop his own horse, led the now-calmed *Colorado* down the road to the pasture for the night.

The next day and for days after, Bill listened to the recounting of the story, not without detectable enjoyment but with absolutely no recollection of the experience itself. He realized that Goyito had saved his life.

They don't make *sabaneros,* or friends, like that anymore. For me, that anonymous, gray concrete statue at the entrance to Liberia does not commemorate a generic Guanacaste cowboy. It is a monument to the nobility of Don Goyo.

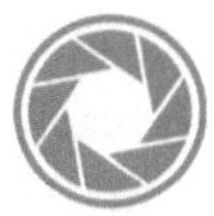

Portrait Mode

Aristides Fulano, A Good Son

Some people leave one or two indelible imprints in the mind's eye as the only available snapshots. That's how I see Aristides and Yolanda, the son and daughter-in-law of Don Alberto and Doña Nita. I have one photo of them together, sitting astride the big wooden gate at the entrance to the corral at San Pascual, the family *finca*. (He had just finished replacing several large fence posts that hold up the barbed wire circling the adjacent pasture. They look happy.)

The one lasting image I have of him, though, is not in a photograph. I see him rolling up to the house in Tempira in 1966 on his gleaming white BMW 500 cc. motorcycle. So quietly, almost stealthy, that machine purred, unlike other Guanacaste motorcycles that putted, spurted, snorted, and made all sorts of other loud noises. This piece of precision engineering seemed to anticipate the ripples, rocks, and gullies in the dirt road and glided over them as though on the German Autobahn. Aristides, though not a tall man, sat tall, his short arms extended full length on the handlebars. It was a gem, and he kept it clean and beautifully polished, the chrome wheel spokes shining brightly. Aristides was a man with laughing eyes, a jester's heart, a beautiful smile, and an ability to hold a poker face only momentarily. Years later he ran into some unexpected financial problems and had to sell the bike back to the bank.

The picture in my mind of Yolanda is that of a youngish but very dour woman dressed completely in black. Even when she wasn't in official mourning, she always seemed to be. Her complexion was lighter than that of most Guanacastecans because, as she constantly used to remind everyone, she was from San Carlos, an inland mountain area close to the capital. Her stare was eerie, unsmiling, between merely intense and mildly demented. Over the years people grew less afraid to say *está loca* (she's crazy) than they were when she was one of the two elementary school teachers and the *directora* of the school. Then everyone gave her proper respect; after all, she was the one with the *preparacion* (schooling). Her clipped speech and melodramatic ways of expressing herself kept townspeople at a distance as she maintained her authoritarian demeanor.

Yolanda scolded the parents almost as much as she did the children. She was incapable of banter or friendly chatting. When Yolanda conversed, she declaimed, orated, lectured, all with melodramatic flourishes of language and stern wagging of her index finger. In less formal conversations, she gave elaborate, repeated, non-stop descriptions of bad or sad things: her mother's afflictions and high blood pressure, her sister's inability to bear up under the burdens of epilepsy, her other sister's madness, and on and on and on until any listener could not help but run out of sympathetic phrases and *ay Dios mio's* (oh, my God) before beginning to shift weight and inch towards the door. *Para no cansarle con el cuento* (so as not to tire you of the story) she'd say, well after you'd already tired. Then she might abruptly change the subject to something more abstract, like decrying the Guanacastecans' "lack of culture," their "*ignorancia*" and lack of "artistic sensibilities."

All these negative aspects she perceived of Guanacaste life made it imperative for her to send their two pretty little daughters, Yolandita and Paulina, to San Carlos to be raised by their grandmother in a "better environment" so they wouldn't wind up marrying Guanacastecos. It always puzzled me that she should find so much fault with Guanacastecos and yet have married one herself. Probably she thought Aristides was different from the usual hard drinking cowboys who worked from 6:00 until lunchtime. And indeed, to many, he was. It was equally puzzling how she could think it was better for her children to be in a house with a bunch of shrouded, misery-ridden *sacos de plagas* (literally, bags of calamities) in

San Carlos instead of in Guanacaste with their father and mother, not to mention the whole extended Fulano family.

Aristides was the "good son" compared with his brother Victor, who had gotten into debt in a misguided joint venture with Danielillo and Armando and wound up living "on the lam" for years in the Limon area, leaving Lupe, his very pretty wife and small son. It was around that time that Aristides sold the BMW, everyone thinks, to help pay his brother's debts. By the time Victor came back Lupe was a little thinner and pale, her pretty face wrinkled, her back slightly bent. She also had two more children, refusing to tell Victor by whom, though most people could guess.

When Victor came back, his parents were not overjoyed. Their shame for his actions outweighed what was left of their love. He had duped them, robbed them, used them, manipulated them. Yet he still expected his mother to wash his dirty clothes by hand because, he said, she got them cleaner than the new little washing machine one of his sisters had just bought for the house. He showed up conveniently at mealtime, yet it never occurred to him to bring even a pound of meat, some neck bones for soup, or some fresh vegetables. He would come in, jocular and jaunty, but immediately turn sullen at his mother's cool greeting. He soon started showing up with his now-teenaged son from another liaison before his marriage to Lupe, thinking the boy could serve as a buffer.

During all those years, Aristides took up the slack for his brother, taking charge of buying, selling, and caring for the cattle with their father at their fince, San Pascual. When Don Alberto no longer could ride out to oversee the work, Aristides went alone with a couple of *peones* then would go into town to do the errands needed by his mother and father before getting back home to Yolanda, who greeted him with her cool sarcasm and jealous slices about his devotion to his parents.

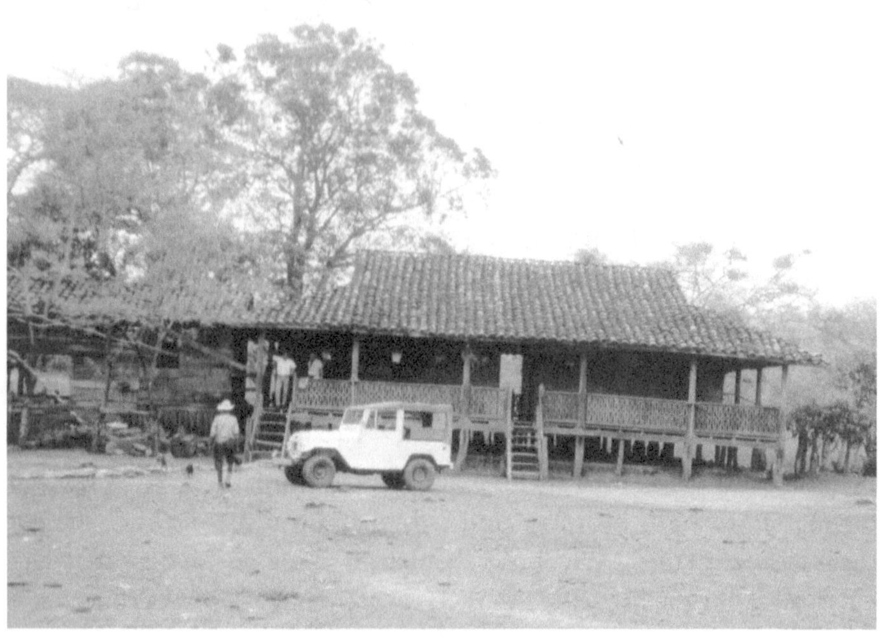

When Don Alberto died, Aristides took over his beloved *macho mula* (mule) that was a bit bigger and more spirited than the other workhorses. With Don Alberto gone, Aristides always made sure that things were repaired and in working order around the house and at the *finca*, because Victor was unreliable, and his sisters and mother couldn't do those things. He would stop by three times a day and often for coffee with his mother who so looked forward to his arrival. Sometimes he would pull her out of her chair and dance a few steps with her to whatever music was coming from the radio or TV. She would say "pshaw" and then almost giggle, as he tried to make her feel happy. Or he'd tell her a story about somebody or something he'd just seen. He once found a little baby parrot that had fallen from its nest at the *finca* and brought it to his mother, and whenever he saw the bird he would jokingly ring out *"Je lorita, 'jueputa lorita"* (hey, little parrot, you son-of-a-bitch!) and wait for his mother's mild *regaño* (scolding) for teaching the bird foul language. *"Ah. Mama, no es nada"* (C'mon, Mama, that's nothing!). Now that it had been more than five years since Don Alberto's death, Doña Nita was beginning to let herself feel happy. She even had begun wearing black and white flecked fabrics in place of her widow's black dresses.

One day in early December Yolanda had gone to San Jose to do some paperwork at the Ministry of Education regarding her retirement. She planned to go on to San Carlos to spend a few days at her sister's and to see her daughters, Yolandita and Paulina. That day Aristides was returning from San Pascual around ten in the morning, having spent the night out there. He was bringing a sack of rice across the top of the *albarda* and the *mula* was trotting along on the gravel and grass shoulder of the two-lane highway, at a perfectly straight part of the road with no trees, no curves, no obstacles. It was a bright sunny morning, one of those December mornings in Guanacaste without a cloud in the sky.

A van carrying six students from the Tropical Studies Institute in San Jose was heading out to a study site in Nicoya. The driver was not from Guanacaste because, as anyone knows who is either a *Guanacasteco* or has lived there for a while, when you see a cow or a horse near the road, with or without a rider, you slow down. You never know what an animal will do. If it gets frightened, it may move in front of a vehicle instead of away from it. The driver of the students' van did not slow down. He was driving very close to the edge of the road, only feet from the mule and Aristides Fulano. The mule suddenly spooked because of the humming motor, and Aristides couldn't rein him back fast enough. The van hit the mule's back legs and threw Aristides off with such force that he ended up on the other side of the road, his neck broken and ribs so splintered that they pierced his lungs, kidneys and liver. He lay there in a pool of blood. The mule writhed in pain and collapsed near the mound of white rice grains from the now-broken sack. The van did not stop.

When help arrived, Aristides was nearly gone, but they took him in an airplane to the hospital in San Jose. He lay in a coma for six days. Aristides had such a strong heart and was so strapping a man even at 54, it took him six days to die. When the accident occurred, a farmhand rushed to the house in Tempira to tell Doña Nita. She had just gotten up from her rocking chair to dust off the plastic table cover to start to set up for lunch, expecting her son to arrive any minute. The morning had awakened with such promise: a grandson was getting a prize at school, her daughter Nuria would be home for the weekend, Christmas was only a few weeks away, and I was coming for the holidays from the Los Angeles.

In an instant the world changed for her, once again. Instead, of seeing her son cheerily arrive she heard the words that transfixed her, that *Aristides fue atropellado. Está por morirse* (that he was struck by a car and was close to death) her first born, her dear Aristides who had been her strength since her husband had gone. There must be a mistake, this can't be, why would God do this? Not her son, why not she herself, dear God? And she wilted on the spot, collapsing onto the nearest chair. By then her daughter Yudit was there. She helped her mother to her room where only moans and sobs "*Dios mio, porque, ay Dios, no puede ser*" (Oh dear God, why, this cannot be) came from them both. Instead of coming home as planned, Nuria went to San Jose to be with Yolanda, who could not be moved from her vigil at her husband's bedside. They both sat for six days and nights, barely eating, barely sleeping, holding his hand, wiping his brow. They were there when he passed.

The same day, Nuria bought a new pair of pants and a white shirt with a little horse's head printed on it for him to be buried in. Three cars had left San Jose for the ride back to the *bajura,* including one car filled with lots of flowers. A caravan of cars met them at the turnoff in Liberia as they drove on to Tempira. At the funeral procession many men wanted to carry Aristides' coffin. It changed supporting arms frequently, not because of the weight, but because everyone wanted a chance to carry him, so beloved was he among the townspeople. Children from the Yolanda's school even formed a noble but rag-tag little color guard to lead the way to the cemetery.

Now several years later, Doña Nita's eyes still fill up with tears when she speaks of her son. He was so good, just in his prime, she says. Doña Yolanda wears her widowhood with a practiced air of authority. Her daughter Yolandita tells me she thinks her mother is crazy because she still fixes meals for Aristides, sets a plate out for him and serves him, then sits at the table and talks to him just as if he were there. Yolandita tells about her mother's behavior with the animation of one relating a movie plot not the death of her father. Her mother, she goes on to say, refused to press charges against the van driver, who was not drunk, just ignorant of the need to slow down when seeing an animal. According to him the mule got in the way of the car. The Tropical Studies Institute had insurance and paid for all the hospital expenses.

Yolanda herself lives almost as though in a trance. She mostly stays inside and writes poetry, though occasionally she goes to Liberia to the poetry society's meetings where she recently won a prize for her work. Sometimes she does a public dramatic reading. Recently she has begun editing a small mimeographed poetry "journal" of contemporary writers. Their late-nineteenth century style, with its images of Parnassus and the Muses, is imitative of the famous Nicaraguan modernist poet Ruben Dario.

Yolandita hardly sees her mother anymore. She married an up-and-coming San Jose lawyer whom no one would ever suspect, much less believe capable, of wife abuse. She is virtually a slave who must ask permission to leave the house and who must rise at 2:00 a.m., or whenever the husband decides to arrive home, to cook his dinner since he flatly refuses to eat anything re-heated or left over from earlier. He beats her often, so that this once pretty girl with long blondish hair and aspirations to be a ballerina and a bilingual secretary now looks haggard and resigned. But not completely, because when she talks her eyes have that same spark that is so reminiscent of Aristides, her father. She told me that she has begun secretly stashing what money she finds in her husband's pockets to sneak away once her own little girl is old enough.

Aristides and Yolanda's younger daughter, Paulina, is also married to a man in San Jose. She graduated from the university with a degree in fine arts but is an unemployed choreographer. She prefers to wear work boots and very skimpy short shorts, especially when she goes back to Guanacaste to oversee her own plot of sugar cane on land her father left her. It has come to most everyone's attention that Paulina works very closely with a muscular, handsome, young Guanacasteco *peon.* Those paying attention to such things even like to point out that she spends more time with him than with her oh-so-suitable San Jose husband.

Occasionally Yolanda visits her mother-in-law, Doña Nita, but confides none too discreetly that she really holds that old woman and her daughters, Aristides's sisters, responsible for his death.

"If he hadn't been so devoted and doing all that work for them he wouldn't have been so tired and would have been more alert to the approaching traffic and could have gotten out of the way on time. But then," she went on to say, "what can you expect from these selfish, ignorant Guanacaste women?"

For the sake of maintaining good family appearances, however, all of them did manage to go together to plant a white plaster cross and name plaque alongside the highway to mark the spot where Aristides lay fatally wounded, only a few yards from another cross remembering another *accidentado*. Before they got back into their red pickup truck, they draped a small halo of pink and purple plastic flowers over the top of the cross. Plastic flowers are better than real ones because they will only fade, not wilt, in the tropical sun

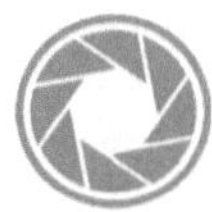

Noise Reduction

Music After Midnight

It's tempting to think that nothing ever changes in a society so rooted in tradition. Each year you see the same people building altars on the street corners for the *Corpus Cristi* Day procession. The old women don't seem to age beyond a certain point. The tranquility of the landscape is unfazed by pavement or a new rice silo or even the sugar refinery smokestacks now spewing large flakes of soot.

But look closely. There are fewer bare-bottomed babies playing in mud puddles near their front stoops. There are more young men herding cattle mounted on motorcycles rather than horses. More young women, instead of aspiring only to motherhood, are taking university classes in Liberia. *Polacos* (the name for mostly-Jewish peddlers) no longer sell cuts of fabric from their pick-up trucks now that ready-made clothing is available. A new breed of traveling salesmen now offers to colorize and update elderly couples' wedding photos. The finished products show a spiffier country couple: the man uncharacteristically dressed in a buttoned shirt, jacket, and Windsor-knotted tie, and both of the pair with lightened complexions. Now they supposedly look more like city folks.

Middle-aged women who remember the old ways fear the loss of "*lo tipico*," (typical) so some still make homemade *tamales* in the backyard and wrap them in fresh banana leaves softened over an open fire. They insist the flavor is different from city-made *tamales* wrapped in aluminum foil. Men now carry plastic water jugs to work, no longer taking the time to whittle and cork round gourds. Now re-usable green or silver Christmas trees with fake snow stand in living rooms instead of the tropical manger scenes with assorted plaster-of-Paris madonnas and faded plastic Disney figurines of Plutos and Mickeys.

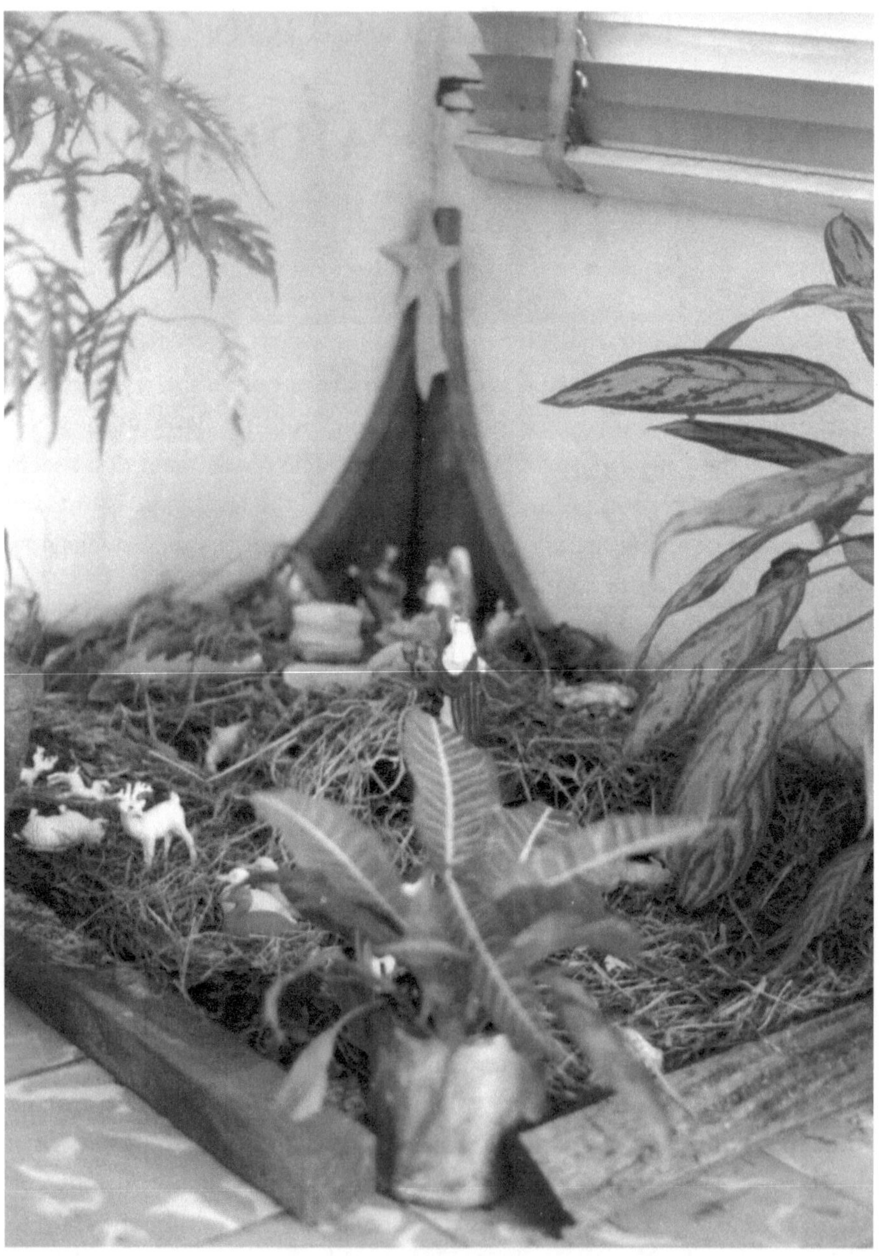

Clinging, clutching to the idea of good olden times while rushing headlong into the future, they cherish, some even covet, blue jeans and color-televised soap operas. Children now know the plots of these complicated melodramas but no longer know the stories and rhymes once considered traditional. Where kids used to create toys from discarded wheel rims, corn silk, and bits of sewing remnants to entertain themselves, now their world includes Ninja Turtles, Barbie, and plastic AKA rifles. And I suppose more recently, the kids might have their noses glued to a cell phone playing online games.

Lamenting change has never done anyone much good. And trying to stop it is as futile as trying to stop the moon from rising. So, I note the seeping, oozing, even predictable changes in Tempira even though most things appear not to change at all. What also becomes apparent to me, however, is the way I see them, for I, too, am evolving, and my dance with Guanacaste still unfolding. I have returned so many times over the years that I hardly experience a tremor where culture shock once was. I am as at home in Guanacaste as in Los Angeles or Tel Aviv, opposites though perhaps not contrary worlds. Invariably, I am pulled back to that place that has been a second home. Had I never gone to Costa Rica, I would not be who I am today, so much did it influence and form me.

By the time I realized that I was neither a visitor nor one who totally belonged there, I was finally able to admit that there are things that really disturb me about some people and life there. I no longer had to be uncritical or to romanticize, overlook, defend, and LIKE everything or everyone. My last extended stay in Guanacaste was a four-month visit in 1983, after three years of graduate folklore studies at UCLA. I went back alone this time. Bill and I had returned to the United States two years earlier. I felt I had been responsible for getting him into that situation nine years before when we took off in the Land Rover for what was to have been only a six-month holiday. I felt morally obligated to get him out as I watched him sink into the numbing world of sloth and alcoholism. We were still married, on paper, but even the friendship was straining. I still thought I could do something to "save" him from himself even though there seemed to be no hope for the relationship. Now that he was back in the U.S. I felt a sense of relief. Before I left on the research trip, I hunted for our Costa Rican marriage documents with the notion of filing divorce.

Being in Guanacaste I am always surprised by my own inability to achieve much in a day. Incidental things like making a phone call or photocopying an article become major tasks to put on a list of "things to do today." For the duration of the four-month research trip, I decided to stay in a hotel room in Liberia and not with friends in Tempira. I needed the privacy to come and go without having to provide explanations or being the subject of neighborly speculations. I needed to be able to read or write without the guilt of appearing to be doing nothing but sitting in a chair. It was a tough decision, but I had to balance those needs with the insult my friends felt at my declining to stay with them.

At the *Hotel Boyeros*, my constant nightly bane was a flashy Wurlitzer jukebox, the same kind of *rocola* that had been so much fun to feed with *pesetas* in Tempira with the other young girls seventeen years before, or to listen to the whiny, romantic laments dedicated to me by the gallant (though tipsy) cowboy everyone protected me against. Now I was approaching middle age and trying to get a good night's sleep so I could get up and do my work the next morning. The *rocola* had lost its charm.

The garbled tones and throbbing rhythms from that gaudy menace mixed with the rowdy laughter of the men rough-housing in the swimming pool outside my cabin room added to the pressure of a vice-grip headache. The jukebox usually came alive soon after dinner and didn't rest until dawn, truly a nocturnal animal whose incessantly wah-wah-wahing saxophones, blaring trumpets, and intense, mechanical percussion controlled the air, preventing even the crickets from owning the night music. Lovely, moonlit, tropical nights with warm westerlies agitating the undulating palm trees may fit someone's romantic image of Guanacaste nights, but that summer I defied anyone to tell me it existed in Liberia, the city that songsters once memorialized as the "white city" with its beautiful *"luna liberiana"* (Liberia moon). I fantasized having the courage to cut the wires or remove a tube from the Wurlitzer's immense cavity, to leave it a mass of non-functioning diodes and colored wires leading nowhere, dependent on a single, missing, and difficult-to-replace component. It would take weeks, hopefully months, to order that piece from Panama, and in the meantime, it would just sit there, impotent in its silence. What a place this is, I remember thinking, a supposedly first-rate hotel where the telephone switchboard works only sporadically, where the bath towels are the size of face cloths, everyone hunts for an ashtray but winds up stomping butts on the floor. There are no drinking glasses or clothes hangers available in the rooms. The soap bars, which are half the size of a soda cracker, are supposed to last a week. And the largest annoyance is the single flashing monster that works unfailingly. It was a torture!

At times I'd get up in the night and plead with the watchman to turn the volume down. If the watchman on duty was an older man, he was sympathetic but powerless because no one listened to him. If the younger watchman was on duty, he only thought I needed someone to accompany me in bed so I'd be diverted from thinking about the noise. Whatever had become of sensuous tropical nights in Tempira when I'd felt surrounded by the star-studded universe and enjoyed the promise of sweet sleep in my safe, mosquito-netted niche? Those delicious nights filled with the sounds of dogs howling, cows lowing, roosters crowing? This version of big city life in the provincial capital of Guanacaste made my apartment in Los Angeles, seem a near bastion of tranquility and thoughtful, considerate neighbors.

During the day, I was embarrassed that I had been making such a fuss over that seemingly petty jukebox. But I never felt truly rested during the whole time I was there. The only thing comparable came several years later when I spent Christmas Eve in Tempira. Magda, the bartender, had hired a *discomovil* to play for a dance in her *cantina*. This was a new experiment, interrupting what used to be the Nazarene quiet of midnight family dinners. I was fully two blocks from the source, yet I would have thought the noise to be coming from the next room. It could not be muffled even if I covered my head with the pillow. The next day, Yolanda, the former school director, who lives across the street from Magda's bar said that the vibrations caused her window panes to shudder, the dining table and chairs to tap dance on the cement floor, and her four-month old granddaughter to shriek with pain until three a.m. She had called the police on several occasions. When they arrived, the music was momentarily lowered, but as soon as they'd gone, it went back to agony-causing decibels. By the time the music stopped, only a handful of people remained in the *salon*. The absence of noise was a relief until we all independently discovered we couldn't hear very well the next day, so sore were our eardrums. I wondered how the creatures with sensitive ears in the surrounding pastures and wooded areas had withstood the noise. Were the hairy tarantulas in the cow pastures suffering uncontrollable urges to dance to the sound waves vibrating their underground nests?

Disease used to plague third-world countries before technological advances became available. Now, one of modernity's additional gifts is runaway, constant racket. Like some of nature's rawest forces, noise has become equally unruly. And while man cannot dominate or control all of Nature's forces, in this case, humans do have the ability to become masters enough of their immediate environment to flick off the switch of what should be only an electronic servant. No one seems to have adopted that concept yet.

Blurred Image

The Gospel According To. . .

Doña Solemne and Don Jose Maria, both quiet and hardworking, are what most people would call "*humilde*" (humble). Today, their small whitewashed cement block house with its roll-out jalousie windows and tiny, mosaic-tiled porch is evidence of their efforts to make a better life for themselves and their family of eight, now all grown up, some with children and even grandchildren of their own. When their children were small, Don Jose Maria and Doña Solemne lived on the same corner in a house about the same size, but one made of irregularly shaped, rough-hewn boards, dark and rotted with years of rain and sun. In spots the boards came unnailed and hung loose, giving the house an unsturdy and ramshackle appearance.

Now, as then, aromatic smoke from the wood stove wafts outward from the kitchen that still faces the street, making it convenient to notice who walks by and with whom. The old floor simply had been tamped dirt which Doña Solemne swept religiously with her broom, basically a large cluster of sticks still bearing their gray-green leaves and tied together with a ragged strip torn from a tattered cotton apron. Today the floor is red ochre-stained concrete and takes a shine with Johnson's paste wax and buffing from the creaky, white string mop. Doña Solemne doesn't own an electric waxer like the neighbors across the way. Her old-style broom is used now only to clear debris from between the small shrubs that stand in orderly rows in front of the house and alongside the raised cement walkway leading the short distance from the street to the front door.

Doña Solemne is a diminutive, slightly paunchy woman. Her shoulders turn downward. Her hair is pulled tightly into a small bun at the back of her head. Her downturned almond-shaped eyes are largely shielded by harlequin-shaped glasses with a greenish tint, giving her lined face an unhealthy pallor. Despite her occasional smiles, she looks wistful and resigned. Her small hands have scrubbed thousands of pounds of laundry and created tens of thousands of tortillas and probably even more *tanelas* (sweet baked corn and cheese with cinnamon cakes). She used to send her kids around town to sell them to augment her husband's *peon's* salary. Don Jose Maria worked hard from dawn until noon, chopping back encroaching vegetation, planting seeds, or loading sand onto a *carreta* with his brother-in-law. After that he would bathe, change his clothes, and relax with his portable radio in the hammock out back. By late afternoon, when it was cooling off, he would chop firewood or make occasional repairs to the barbed wire fence or do other yard work.

A wiry, slender man with a slight limp, Don Jose Maria was chattier than Doña Solemne and stopped frequently along the way to exchange a word of greeting with other men. He was not one to spend hours in the cantina, but some Saturdays he did have one drink too many and spent all day Sunday behind the curtained doorway to the dark bedroom, where no one but a few mosquitoes would bother him. Doña Solemne meanwhile puttered with her plants, cooked, mended clothes, shooed chickens from inside the house and always had a fresh fruit drink ready for any visitor who might drop by. In the years when her children were small the older ones were in charge of the little ones and were often seen around the yard or in the dusty road dragging or hoisting one of the placid, bare-bottomed toddlers with snot-stained faces. There were strong family resemblances among them all, though one of the girls was cross-eyed.

Every third Sunday afternoon the Spanish priest came to Tempira to say Mass. Later he starting coming every week and was also available if someone paid for a special Mass to mark the anniversary of a loved one's death. There's a reduced rate for more than one honoree. Often people pay for a whole year at a time so the priest will come on same day each month.

Doña Solemne and Don Jose Maria were one of the only couples in Tempira who attended church more or less together. She sat with her three sisters well near the front so she could join in the singing. He was responsible for ringing the bells announcing the mass. He would begin fifteen minutes before the designated hour, then five minutes, then finally when the priest had arrived and the Mass was about to begin, which might be up to a half hour after the time originally scheduled. Once the Mass began Don Jose Maria stood at the doorway with some of the other men who rarely entered further than the back rows, preferring the large empty space just inside the door. They neither sang nor kneeled nor repeated the prayers responsively, but they did cross themselves and kiss their thumbs at the appropriate moments. Don Jose Maria was one of the few men who almost always took communion when it was offered.

Don Jose Maria was more demonstrably religious than most of the other men. The majority stayed home on Sundays, but some just hung out at Mariela's *cantina* across the street, drinking while waiting for the woman in their life to come out of the church. They seldom crossed the line between the holy and secular worlds except when some church repair or construction took place. The men planted shrubs, laid concrete sidewalks, or fixed leaks in the roof. Once they brought ladders and built scaffolding to help scrub the walls of the church. That was when it was still brand new fifteen years earlier just before Christmas. It was the day after Juancito, Doña Mencha's son, had put a .22 pistol in his mouth and pulled the trigger, ending his days of despair after his girlfriend told him she was going off with another. His blood and brains were spattered on the wall over the wooden crucifix and pieces even sprayed onto the back wall. The whole place had to be scraped and repainted in time for holidays. Many of the men helped out then.

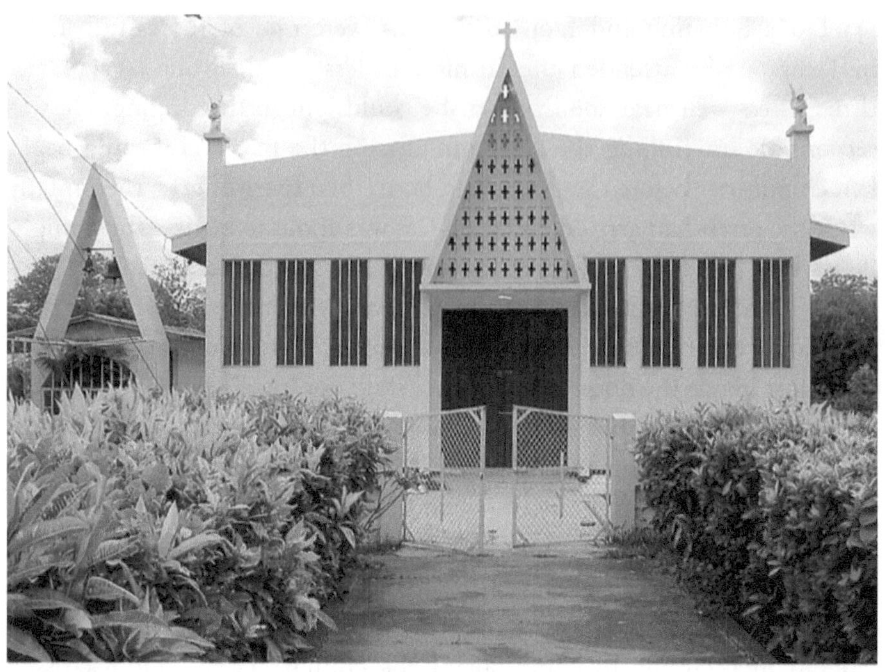

Doña Solemne was so devoutly religious that sometimes she would wear a brown habit-like dress with a long apron and a large wooden rosary to show her appreciation to or ask a favor from *San Francisco*, her favorite. The bib portion of the apron was fitted with a square plastic pocket protecting a pale blue and brown image of *San Francisco*. More than once she had petitioned the saint to spare the life of one of her babies suffering from a high fever or uncontrollable diarrhea. Then there was the time when her teenage son, Beto, began drinking heavily. She promised *San Francisco* this extra devotion if only he would intercede to help make Beto stop drinking. Sometimes Doña Solemne dressed like that for several months; sometimes for a specific amount of time: commonly forty days. The long-sleeved heavy cotton dress with its several layers of modest ornamentation was truly penitential in the steamy, blisteringly hot sun that pierces every unshaded spot in Tempira. Doña Solemne, however, looked tranquil and like her name, solemn, in her nun-like garb. Whether or not such behavior extended within the confines of her bedroom is something only she and Don Jose Maria know, of course. Maybe this was an agreed-upon way of preventing the large family from getting still larger.

One day I stopped by to visit Doña Solemne during my visit in 1991. I hadn't seen her for ten years. The only difference I noted in her appearance was that where before a few broken and jagged teeth had dotted her otherwise bare gums, she now had a full set of straight white teeth, another sign of a better life. She smiled and invited me to sit and drink some fresh lemonade, saying she was happy to see me. When I asked about Don Jose Maria, though, her faced stiffened, and she began to fill up with tears which she tried unsuccessfully to hold back. I was afraid she was going to tell me he had died. But she swallowed her tears and lifted her head in a slightly disdainful manner, turning at that moment towards the window near where we were seated.

"Ay, Doña Susana, something worse than death. He's up the street at the *culto* -- he's become an *evanqelico* (Evangelical born-again Christian). Those people are everywhere. They're a *plaga* (plague). They've taken my husband; he was such a good Catholic. They've broken up families all over the place and eaten up all their spare time. Can you imagine, after all those years of hard work? How we struggled together to raise our children and build this house. I never dreamed we wouldn't be old together if we were both alive. Now, look, here I am, alone, while he's up the street there singing with those folks every spare minute. And do you know what's the worst part? Now there's no chance that we'll be together in eternity after we die." Her voice was nearly a whisper.

"And there's nothing I can do. They've got him."

She lifted her gaze to look me straight in the eye and held tightly to the both hands I had offered her. She blinked back the tears, quietly lamenting the eternal loneliness awaiting her.

Controlling the Composition

Wealth Redistribution

My best friend Ana's older brother, Eddy, was twenty-seven when he married perky, sweet fourteen-year-old Haydee. Her finely chiseled features and light-hearted manner gave her a princess-like quality. Seldom was she seen wielding the wet mop or running errands to her grandmother's house like her older sister was required to do. Occasionally she might play out in front with one of her twin younger brothers, Jesus and Cesar, but usually they had each other's company and didn't cling to Haydee for attention. Even on the warmest days, pretty little Haydee seldom seemed uncomfortable, hardly perspiring from doing an occasional chore or errand, which always fell to the others anyway. She was so pretty that everyone seemed to pamper her as if awed her good looks.

Getting married at fourteen was not unusual when her grandmothers were young, but not many fathers were willing to marry off their daughters quite that young anymore. Since the 1970s, with the highway completed and a branch of the university only thirty kilometers away, there were other options even for country girls from humble families. They could finish high school and become provisional teachers or attend university classes to study education or social work. The more serious (and affluent) girls might continue their studies in San Jose and look forward to becoming pharmacists or lawyers.

But the opportunity to marry Haydee into the Fulano family was too tempting for Haydee's father to pass up. He knew that his daughter wasn't too interested in studying, so why not marry money? Unless she went to San Jose to work, she probably would not find anyone nearby who could raise her status, (and his!!), as much as Ana's brother. And how else would a bony, unattractive, braggart like Eddy be able to find anyone as pretty and pliant as sweet little Haydee? His less-than-handsome face and rail thin, scrawny body, made him a perfect mama's boy with a crackling voice and a cockiness that gave the muscular *peones* and *sabaneros* cause for much derisive laughter. Eddy used to show off on a Sunday morning or in the early evenings by careening around the town square on a large, noisy NFK motorcycle, often standing up on the seat, trying to keep his balance while making sure that bigger guys playing pool or drinking in the *cantina* saw him go by. A few years later, he learned to pilot small planes and got a job with the local crop dusters. Swooping and tipping his wings low over his family's house after each turn around a cotton or rice field, he caused his mother a lot of hand wringing and *ay-yay-yay*ing anxiety. She feared that he would crash into the trees and die in a burning heap of wreckage right before her eyes. None of the girls near his own age were much impressed by his *payasadas* (clowning), but to someone as young as Haydee, his antics were funny and heroic, and his attentions romantic. As Haydee's first suitor, Eddy could prop up his weak ego knowing that she had not yet known any others' embraces. Or had she?

Haydee's father, Alejandro, who earned his meager living helping his own father load and drive an ox-cart, had merchant ambitions. After delivering his daughter in perfect, untouched condition to the altar where Eddy waited for his bride, Alejandro was positioned and ready to reap all the rewards from the new family ties.

That was the unwritten part of the deal. With his low-key and pseudo-servile, courteous manner, he was able to convince his daughter's new mother-in-law to set him up with a little *pulperia* (general store) and to give him a house and a pasture. In less than a year after the marriage, Alejandro began to peacock around as a merchant in a clean, pressed shirt and closed shoes instead of the old rubber boots and mud-and-dung-spattered work clothes of an ox-cart driver.

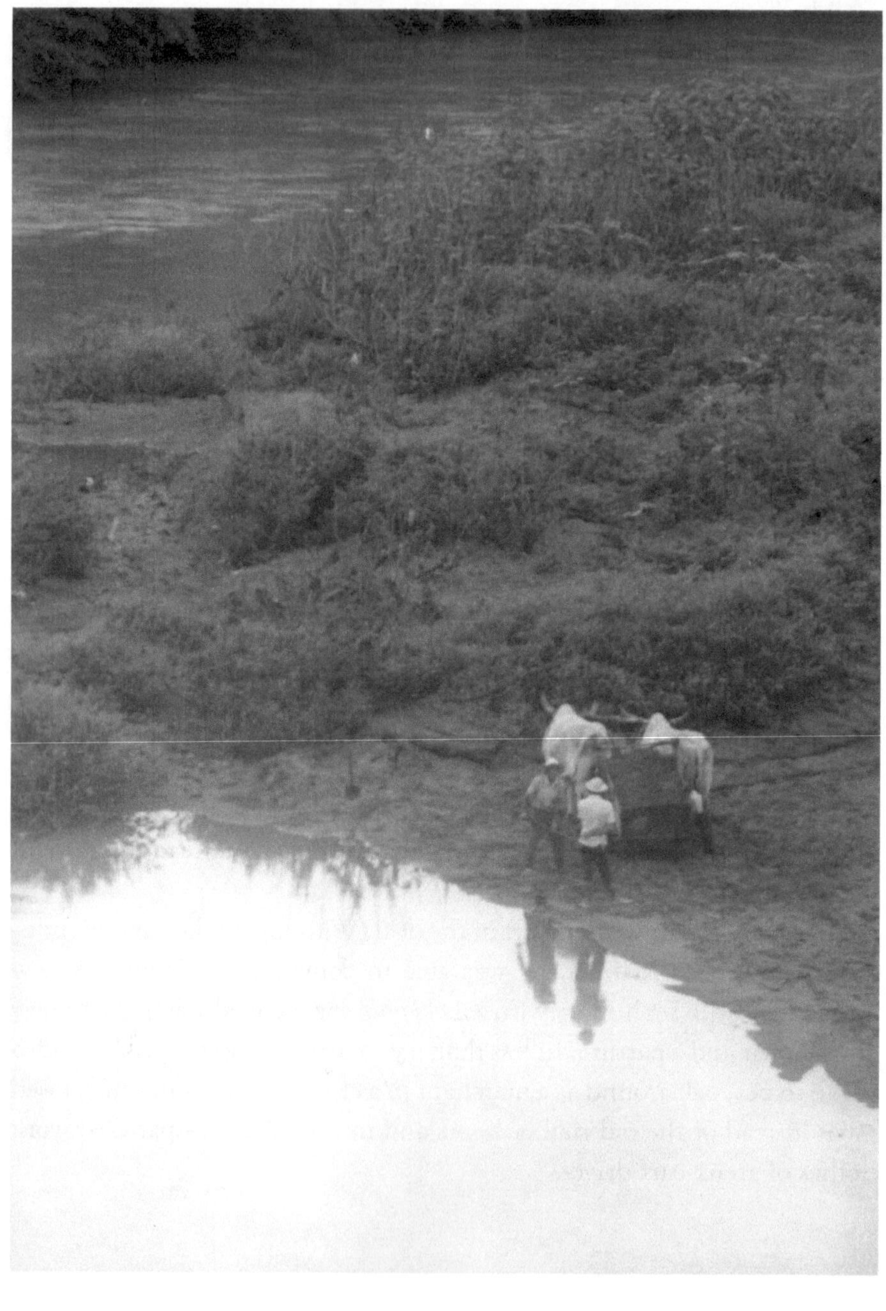

Now he wore a big gold ring with a square-cut red stone on his pinky and after-shave cologne on his closely shaven jaw. He waited on his customers, mostly youngsters or ladies who bought the urgent miscellanies of the day -- a cylindrical bar of blue laundry soap (years before there were plastic bags of detergent powder), a meter of pastel *docoma* (a synthetic fabric) for a new blouse, a half pound of sugar for *limonada* or other fruit drink, two eggs, a tomato, and a couple of chocolate covered liquor-filled candies called *guaritos* and later, when he got a refrigerator, a half pint of *natilla* (sour cream), an ice cream bar, or even a frozen chicken. From behind the glass and wood showcase-counter, he stood adding aloud columns of figures awkwardly scrawled on the top sheet of thin brown wrapping paper. Alejandro was in the ideal spot to overhear all the latest gossip being exchanged without ever having to change his placid expression or appear interested. He faked graciousness in the dark little wood-floored store, knowing it was better than being out in the sun, dust, and wind or rain. No more of that poking and coughing out "*Jooocha*!" to stir lethargic, neutered beasts to their feet, and struggle to yoke them to their creaky unpainted ox-cart. Ox-carts in Guanacaste are pale and rustic compared with those famous brightly painted souvenir versions of the national icon sold at every tourist shop in San Jose. (In Spanish the word for yoke is *yugo*. A *conyuge* is a couple of yoked oxen. It is probably no accident that *conyuge* also means married couple, sharing the Latin root with the English word "conjugal," so often followed by bliss. In this family scene, the real bliss most assuredly belonged to Alejandro.)

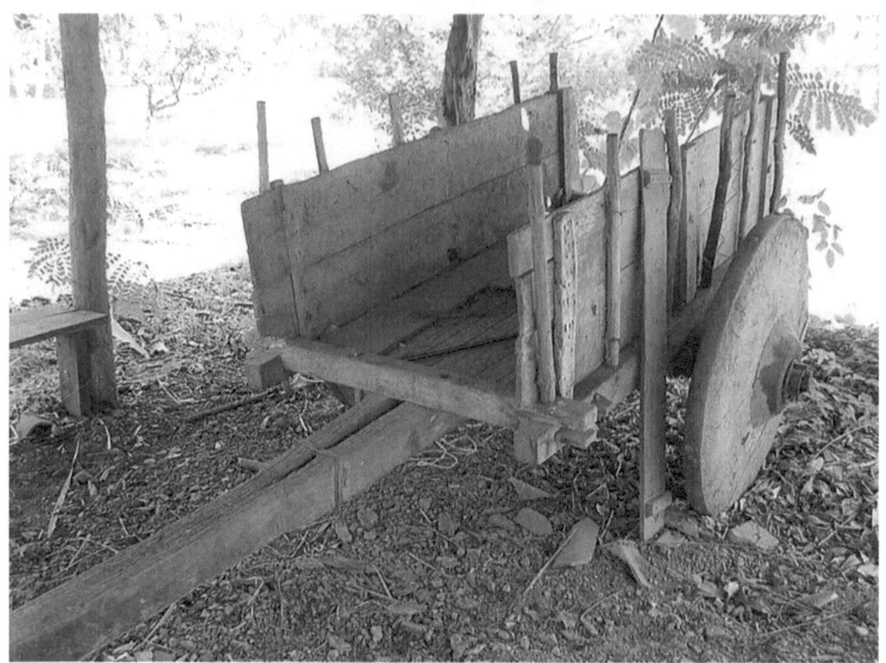

It wasn't long before Haydee, now *la señora de Fulano* began putting on airs and dressing and making up well beyond her years. At sixteen she could easily pass for twenty-five. Eddy sometimes allowed her to walk the block and a half to visit her mother, although more often he drove her in his latest Toyota sedan or jeep, stirring up dust with abrupt starts and screeching brakes on the way. The embarrassed look on Haydee's face suggested that some of the boyish charm of those formerly-funny antics had already worn thin. Except to go to her mother's house, Haydee was not permitted to go anywhere else alone. Her sister and twin brothers occasionally visited. Over the next six years, she had four children, all of whom looked like their father. None of them physically resembled Haydee, for which she was more grateful than sorry. If any of the children had not strongly resembled Eddy, he might have been more severe in his constant badgering and jealous controls. But the children did learn their mother's guile and wiles.

The years have been physically very good to Haydee. Unlike many other Guanacastecan women who have had four children, she has not grown plump and fatigued. In fact, her good looks showed no signs of tarnish or tawdriness until fairly recently, but it would be difficult to claim the hardships of motherhood as the cause.

She began spending part of her time in Tempira and part in a beautiful home Eddy bought in San Jose with some questionably-obtained funds. When in the capital, she was securely and comfortably installed behind the double set of decorative iron gates, overseeing several servant girls from Guanacaste whom she recruited away from their mothers on the condition that she would make sure they took night classes in a nearby high school and not allow them to go out alone with men.

Even though Haydee enjoyed the luxuries of the higher status, she was not like the real society ladies in San Jose, who go to teas, bridal showers or charity lunches for the local hospital or other charities. She was not especially interested in reading unless it was a beauty magazine to learn about the newest colors in eye shadows or some extravagantly painted and jeweled fingernail designs. For her, serious reading was a romance *photonovela*, a comic book-like magazine with blocks of photographed characters playing out a soap-opera-esque story line.

Over the years Haydee lost any traces of genuine sweetness and began to exude a saccharine quality that oozed from the pores of her near-model-perfect face. Her sparkling eyes and dentist's-pride smile belied an almost pathological yet subtle capacity for cruelty towards Ana, her sister-in-law. Haydee gets her own way, always, with her husband, and she has little difficulty convincing him of whatever she sets her mind to inventing about anyone, usually his own sister. Over the years Haydee had remarkably clever excuses for not helping take care of her in-laws when they began to need care as they still lived in Tempira. For instance, she refused a plea from Ana who phoned her from San Jose requesting that she drop next door to help their mother insert a contact lens after cataract surgery. Haydee might have refused because she was afraid, but the reason she gave was that she would have to file down her fingernails in order to do so. She then convinced Eddy and his mother that it was Ana's innate selfishness that was at the heart of her unwillingness to make the four-hour drive to Guanacaste from San Jose, to perform this task herself. Repeated instances of similar condemnations kept Ana on guard during any socializing she was forced to endure with Haydee, who had artfully refined her ability to utter insults and blow kisses with the same breath.

One morning, a few years later, Ana called Haydee and Eddy in Tempira, telling them to come to San Jose immediately because their mother had unexpectedly suffered a heart attack and died just before 6:00 that morning. Both parents by then had been living in Ana's house in San Jose because it was the only way she could take care of them and manage her own home. Ana told me about that awful day her mother passed, how in the intervening hours, she had had to administer her invalid father's diabetes medicine, bathe him and break the news to him that his wife of over sixty years, but ten years his junior, had just died. She also had to go to town to get a death certificate signed, arrange for a casket, the priest and services, and funeral car to go to Guanacaste the same day for a late afternoon burial. It is customary to bury the dead in Guanacaste within twenty-four hours because of the hot climate and lack of mortuary practices. She then dedicated herself to bathing and dressing her mother's body. She operated in a state of shock but managed to carry out all the necessary tasks with no help or support from anyone other than her nine-year-old son, Milton.

When Haydee and Eddy arrived five hours later after a plane ride from Guanacaste, Haydee displayed her "grief" by observing disdainfully that Ana had neglected to put lipstick and rouge on her dead mother's face. She remarked accusingly and without the slightest hesitation that Ana never did like to see her mother looking nice so that must be why she hadn't put lipstick on her. Over the next several hours, Haydee exercised her viper-like charm, convincing Eddy that Ana, who had solely cared for their aging parents, had been neglectful of their mother. According to her, this sudden death could only be Ana's fault and that, in fact, she should be taken to court and accused of murder. Haydee took it upon herself to carry this tale back to Tempira with a zealot's determination even in time for the burial. She spared no details as she fabricated them on the spot for anyone willing to listen, which many did because it gave them a chance to tsk-tsk between their mournful sobs, even as they walked behind the casket in the 5:00 p.m. procession to the cemetery. But Haydee's credibility had already begun slightly to falter, even among Ana's usual detractors who had always not-so secretly considered her too liberal, too urban, or too uppity, an educated Guanacasteca who had abandoned her rural roots.

It seems that over the years Haydee's more flexible living arrangements permitted her a multitude of entertainment possibilities that many less attractive, harder working mothers of four did not enjoy. The novelty of being married to Eddy had long ago worn thin. She was bored with him and not surprisingly, felt unexcited about her life. At twenty-four, Haydee became aware of what she was missing in her life when she discovered a French film called *Emmanuelle* that was playing at a local theater in San Jose. Rather than create a family scandal and hardship by leaving Eddy and the financial security that the relationship provided her (and her family), she prevailed upon Eddy to find some more interesting ways of satisfying some of her (and apparently his) unmet needs.

Haydee convinced Eddy to invite that handsome weightlifter, German, from Heredia who worked at a local ranch in Guanacaste to participate in recreating some scenes from *Emmanuelle* that Haydee had found compelling. The ranch administrator was fair-skinned and blue-eyed, and being widely known as a lady's man and a hustler. He was willing to do most anything, more so if it involved money. The story has it that he spent afternoons with Haydee and Eddy engaging in whatever forms of erotic posturing they paid him for. The problem came, of course, when the fee did not include his silence, and he chose to tell more than a few people about being propositioned by Eddy Fulano who was seeking to mollify his wife, and in effect admitting to his own failings. The genial, muscular playboy, who himself was married to a former San Jose beauty-queen-turned-resentful-matron and had two young teenagers, pretended to be shocked and surprised but admitted laughingly and quite unabashedly to allowing himself to be hired. That he might disappear from work for hours on end was never seriously questioned. Ranch supervisors spend a lot of time in their little pick-up trucks running errands to the bank, buying and loading sacks of fertilizers and feed, picking up spare parts for broken tractors, arranging deliveries to the rice mill or the cattle slaughterhouse, looking for crop-dusters or cane-cutters, and, of course, stopping for "just one" beer with whoever is inviting. Stopping for quick passionate encounters was not out of the ordinary either. Lunch hour coincides with the hottest part of the day, so not much work can be done anyway until 3:00 when the workers return for an overtime session. So even though the schedule seems busy, there is always time to indulge in life's simple pleasures and gifts. And if it meant a little supplemental income in addition, better still.

Haydee was closing in on thirty-five. Her youngest was almost fifteen; the oldest just out of college. Her father and mother still owned and ran the little store next door to a comfortable white-washed home with red trim they built. Much of the land that had belonged to Haydee's mother-in-law was passed through Eddy's signature directly to Haydee's father. Don Alejandro, as he was now respectfully called. He had offered, and for some reason Eddy accepted, a price way below market value for 200 acres of the original family ranch that Eddy's father had given him to work years ago. The two houses which Haydee and Eddy lived in were both in her name now, as well. One of her twin brothers, Jesus, now owned the house that Ana's mother had originally built for Eddy back when she hoped he would take over the little ready-made clothing shop she ran. His mother never liked his flying and used to pray fervently to Saint Anthony, whose picture hung on her bedroom wall, to put some sense into that boy's head. The pasture land that Ana's 94-year-old father still owned was to be divided, when he died, between Ana and Eddy, but no one would be surprised if and when they see Don Alejandro getting out of his double-cabin pick-up to open the gate for a hired ranch hand to move some cows in or out of Eddy's portion of the pasture one day.

Around that same time, Eddy gave up crop dusting. He insisted that twenty years of breathing parathion, malathion, and a complete menu of other Bayer and Dow chemical products had nothing to do with his decision to call it quits. It just got boring, and besides no one was paying much attention anymore or wringing her hands in worry whether he tipped his wings one way or the other or swooped low over the trees in Tempira. Certainly, Haydee was not entertained by those old antics. Some days he could be seen occasionally riding a bicycle along the newly-paved street in town. He had to sell the house in San Jose, and no longer had any land to rent or farm. Most of the time he stayed at home.

Even though they only lived two hundred meters from the cemetery, in a beautiful new home he had built on the outskirts of town, neither Haydee nor Eddy ever thought to put some fresh flowers on his mother's grave. Nor did he ever offer to share the costs for the monthly anniversary mass that the priest celebrated during the first year after her death. He and Ana rarely spoke to each other except to discuss something relating to the remaining land in their father's estate. Ana even stopped hoping that he would send money to share with the expenses of medicating their ailing father, which was running over $200 a month.

Eddy and Haydee rarely went into town. Word had it *("dice la gente")* that the young fair-skinned, college-aged son of one of Ana's cousins has been seen visiting quite regularly with Haydee and her husband, who was learning to use his new home video camera and recorder. Eddy also had bought a closed van that is outfitted for trips to the beach on moonless nights. What goes on in the van is no longer much of a secret because many men will laughingly boast about having been invited on such outings. It had become a way for a nearly-bankrupt Eddy to buy some time from his creditors or make favorable new deals while voyeuristically enjoying what other men did with his wife. Even some married women spoke indignantly about how he suggested to their husbands that they leave their children at home and go as a couple to the beach for some fun with him and Haydee. One couple, not knowing ahead of time what was going on, did go. They didn't get the picture until the drinks were flowing, the salsa music was playing on the portable tape player, and Haydee began unbuttoning her blouse, revealing her bare breasts as she leaned over in rhythm to the music to rub snakily against the other woman's husband and run her fingertips suggestively on his thigh.

> For years, Ana refused to believe these stories, considering them products of those envious, malicious gossip-mongers who thrive on lying about others. But then, she began to believe them as even trusted friends talked about Haydee. 'There's not much to say, really" Ana lamented, " except, well, what can you expect? Her father was the first to sell her, so why wouldn't she allow her husband to do so also?"

This story was going to end here. But then I got a letter from Ana in 1998. Eddy had gone back to crop dusting. She wrote to tell me that she had received a call from the police in Tempira, that Eddy's plane had crashed into the trees. He died in a burning heap of wreckage, his body charred beyond recognition. "At least," Ana said, "it wasn't right before our mother's eyes."

Double Exposure

Todos Somos Iguales

"I didn't sleep with you last night so why aren't you saying *'Buenos Dias* (Good Morning)?"

One learns manners quickly in Guanacaste with a reminder like that! No one lets you get away with showing up at the breakfast table and not making proper acknowledgement of the new day. Saying "*Buenos Dias*" or "*Como amaneció*?" (literally, how did you wake up?) is as important as asking permission to take leave ("*con permiso*") with the response "*Propio*" or "*Suyo*" (Yours). Being polite means not only greeting people when you enter a room, but also when you get on a bus, saying hello to the driver but loudly enough for other passengers to return the greeting, and saying "adios" to people passing on the street.

Even non-Spanish speakers know that "*adios*" means good bye, but in the sense of "farewell" if someone is leaving for a long time or for good. Less permanent "good byes" are Hasta Luego, Hasta Pronto, Hasta Mañana, Nos Vemos, Ciao, even, more recently Bye-bye. So, strange as it may seem, "*adios*" is also used to mean "hello." It can be said with an exaggerated drawl among friends or in flirtation, "*Aaaahhdioooooos*") or just matter-of-factly " *'dioj*" as is customary when passing anyone along the way in the street in Tempira and other small towns. Everyone knows everyone else, so it's just courtesy to acknowledge their existence even if you don't want to stop and chat. Unless there's some reason to snub someone, it's considered rude to ignore him because that implies that you are *creida*, (snobby, thinking yourself superior).

Being *creida* is something very much frowned upon in this country where people frequently tell you *"todos somos iguales"* and will enforce this in socially insignificant but often personally harmful ways. Someone who seems to have gotten "too big for her britches" may have the "floor lowered from underneath" her. *Bajarle el piso* is a practice occurring on all social levels, even among university professors. For instance, there was the case of a university department head who had just received an honor for publishing an article and was feeling proud of her accomplishment. Colleagues made sure she didn't feel so good that she would think herself better than the others (who hadn't done anything close to noteworthy in years). Even my supervisor at the university did that to me after I'd finished a Masters degree in folklore studies by saying "Oh, so now you're a big expert in witchcraft, eh?" rather than even the basic "congratulations, good work!"

That malicious leveling technique is seen a lot, too, if someone is envious of another's new outfit, appearance, or new possession. Rather than being happy for a woman who looks especially attractive in a new outfit, it is often more usual to *chotear* (make fun of) her, or try to make her feel self-conscious by telling her the dress is a strange color or a peculiar cut, anything to make her not want to wear the garment again and think she looks good. Or they might engage in what is commonly called an *indirecta*, (indirect criticism), in which two people will talk insultingly about a third who is actually present but not included in the conversation. This often happens while shopping for a few things in the *pulperia* or standing on line in the morning waiting for bottles of fresh milk. An example of an *indirecta* is sarcastically saying to the person next to you, "Oh, why don't you put on some shorts so you can look as pretty as someone over there who shows off everything, walking around so provocative and thinking she looks so pretty?"

Not being better than others, by the way, is hailed by many Costa Ricans as integral to what their democracy is all about. If someone feels better (or smarter, more accomplished, superior in any way) it means that we are not all equal, and that must be remedied. Maintaining the lowest common denominator takes precedence over and actually undermines any striving for excellence. Small wonder that Costa Ricans of truly great achievement, be it a teenaged violinist, a scientist, or a sports figure, often leave to live in Europe, Mexico, or the U.S.

On the other hand, people in Guanacaste tend to look down on those, especially foreigners, who look like they're "slumming," trying to look lower or poorer than the poorest by wearing dirty or torn shirts, ripped jeans, shoes with holes or going barefoot in town. After all, everyone knows it costs money to travel to another country, so these visitors MUST have enough money to dress nicely and cleanly. Looking sloppy is simply seen as being disrespectful and insulting. It is even worse to be considered dirty. Once a student of mine wrinkling his nose in disgust as he told me about a Russian friend of his who wears the same underwear several days in a row. (How he knew this I have no idea!). A Guanacasteca living in San Jose used to make fun of the woman who cleaned her house, an older lady from Cartago, who didn't bathe very often and exuded a strong body odor. She used to refer to as "*Doña Tufa*" (Mrs. Stinky) instead of referring to her by her name.

Admittedly I, too, came to view European and American travelers with the same skepticism as many Costa Ricans. It's easy to feel critical, almost contemptuous, towards, but more, embarrassed, by those foreigners who seem oblivious to local manners and appropriate dress. I snobbishly wanted to distance myself from them out of fear that their behavior would be deflected onto me and I'd be identified as one of them.

Unless you go to resort areas or frequent hotels or restaurants along the Interamerican Highway in Guanacaste, it's easy to avoid seeing most tourists. But one holiday afternoon I found it unavoidable. That day I was returning from Liberia on the 3:00 bus. I had missed the 2 o'clock bus by a minute, so I had whiled away the hour across the street on a park bench. At 2:45 I decided to wander, over and get on line at the crowded open-air bus terminal. The midday *tope de caballos* (procession of fancily arrayed horses and riders) was over, and now the *cantinas* were packed, music and spirits flowing. Young people were strolling in the street, the girls often with linked arms. Many were headed out to the *Camera de Ganaderos* (cattle grange grounds) for the livestock show and to get good seats for the salsa/ rock concert of *La Banda*, then the hottest group in San Jose. Some children carrying triangular blue, white, and red banners (the colors of the Costa Rican flag) and tooting paper noisemakers toddled along after their mothers. I boarded the bus and sat pressed against the window on the red vinyl seat over the wheel well, my knees practically touching my chest. There were two other people squeezed with me onto the seat that was built comfortably for two. I recognized the man sitting next to me as one who had ridden into town on the same bus with me a few hours earlier. The driver was in the narrow aisle, helping an elderly *campesino* stash his cardboard-boxed purchases on the narrow overhead rack. A young woman nudged two of her children along the aisle looking for seats. In one arm she held an infant wrapped in pink flannel, and from the other hung a plastic woven shopping sack filled with vegetables and other staples she had just bought at the market.

Ducking under the arms of people in the aisle was a ten-year-old boy with a tray fashioned from a shallow cardboard box hanging from his neck by several strands of cotton string. The tray was filled with the squares of *cajeta* (cinnamon, brown sugar and evaporated milk fudge-like candies) his mother had made that morning and sent him out to sell. He turned sideways and grabbed the box with both hands to avoid spilling the sweet squares as someone from inside the bus decided to leave.

Outside, some men standing on line had the glassy-eyed expression of those whose heads are swimming from too much alcohol. Along one side of the bus a man with one arm amputated at the elbow was barking his sing-song pitch with near operatic *brio* "*Numeros, compre pedazos de loteria*" to sell lottery tickets before tomorrow's drawing. On the other side of the bus was the man with his shaved-ice cart, shouting *granizados!* (ices) as he rasped at the huge block of ice set in his painted cart. He filled paper cones, pouring red liquid sugar from large liquor bottles over the ice. As an added treat and for only a few cents extra, he would also pour condensed milk over the top. Several people were waiting for him and a couple of girls inside the bus leaned out the window with their coins as he passed their ice cones up to them.

Nearly a month had passed with no rain. The day was hot and muggy, and arms and faces were sweaty and still wet from the quick rain shower which had caught everyone unprepared. A couple of teen-aged boys in the back of the bus played a transistor radio at high volume which mixed with the profusion of music from the refreshment establishments all around the terminal area. From the street came the sound of a crackling loudspeaker with music blaring from a passing car. Out of the car window a man with a bullhorn shouted, inviting people out to the fair grounds for more celebration activities later that evening.

From my seat several rows behind the driver, I noticed a family of North American travelers, a couple in their late thirties with two children about seven and ten edging towards the head of the line to board the bus. They all carried bulky backpacks strapped on. As they made abrupt turns to talk with one another maneuvering themselves through the throngs, they bumped people aside who were also trying to get on line. The woman seemed to be the only one of the four who spoke some Spanish. Her hair looked greasy and tangled, as though she hadn't washed or combed it for days. She wore a pair of baggy, olive drab short shorts and a wrinkled V-neck halter top of the same color. It was loosely tied, so that her sagging bra-less breasts were visible to anyone who happened to glance her way.

Now she stood blocking the doorway as she tried to get directions from the bus driver. People inside and outside the bus were staring at the halter-topped *gringa* as she pushed her way up the stairs into the bus to show the driver a map of Guanacaste and to ask if this bus would take her where she wanted to go. The driver was distracted by the hubbub, but since it was nothing out of the ordinary, he maintained a relative calm that was quite admirable. While he was not much interested in the map that she had shoved in his face with a rather imperial flourish, he tried to reassure her that this bus would, indeed, take them to a place where they could catch another bus to Samara beach, their final destination. As she turned quickly to motion to her husband and kids to board behind her, her heavy backpack whacked the shoulder of a young girl who was trying to step around her. The remaining folks on the line deferentially cleared the way for the family as they butted in front without so much as saying "excuse me." Once inside the bus, they moved proprietarily toward the remaining two rows of empty seats, never once making eye contact with anyone already seated.

Her voice somehow managed to rise above all the bus station cacophony "OK, look, we're going to have to sit apart, kids. Jesse, Jennifer you sit here, no, no, not there, right here." Her voice boomed like a Marine staff sergeant's, and suddenly there was a hush inside the bus except for the tinny music from the boys' transistor radio. I turned my head slightly and saw passengers looking up to the ceiling or out the windows or straight ahead. Two teen-age girls in front of me with bejeweled plastic butterfly clips holding their hair in place cupped their hands to whisper something and giggled while looking up at this dirty-blond Amazon in their midst. The family had commandeered two full rows for themselves and their backpacks. The woman leaned over to try to open the window next to her children, but at that angle it was practically impossible. She stood up on the seat in her dirty sandals to try forcing it down with more of her weight. The younger child, the little girl, not yet seated, eyed the lady in front of her with a look of disgust and said quite loudly "Euuuuww, Mommy, why does that lady smell like that?" She was apparently sensing the odor of *brillantina*, a hair grooming lotion that many people used to keep their curly hair from fluffing in the wind. The lady herself looked as though she had only minutes before just stepped out of the shower; her pink-flowered dress was crisply pressed and she mopped her perspiring face every few minutes with a clean white handkerchief.

"Just shut the fuck up, Jenny. Sit down. Here, do you want a banana or some grapes?"

Her husband for the first time piped up, "Oh Sal, you didn't buy fruit from that dirty stand, did you? It's probably not even organically grown. Are you sure that that guy was listening to you when you asked him directions to the beach? Go ask him again."

All the passengers were more or less settled into their seats. The last people on line had just boarded and were making their way with their bags and boxes toward the back of the bus or to any seat that only had two people. They moved closer together to make room for a newcomer who might now only get to have one "cheek" well placed if the other two seat companions were hefty. Sal took her map, got up, and pushed against the flow. It wasn't hard to see the dirt under her fingernails and the concentric rings of dirt and dust mixed with sweat around her sunburned neck. She shouted with a tone of desperation in very broken Spanish to the driver, "Hespera, seenyor, estar usted segura que esta es correcto bus para nosotros ir al playa esta en mapa?"

The teen-age boys lowered the volume on their radio to listen to her brand of Spanish and in a softer but audible voice tried playfully to imitate it to each other. The driver pulled the cord to sound the low, throaty horn, resembling something between a lovesick cow and a factory whistle. The boys bellowed an imitation of that sound, too, and some people laughed, comic relief, while others just looked embarrassed. The driver turned and looked a little rattled, for the first time, perhaps because the boys were mocking his bus or because the *gringa* was still doubting his word. *"Si, senora. Por favor, sientase. Yo Ie aviso, no se preocupe.* (Yes, ma'am, please sit down, I'll let you know, don't worry.) She turned to go back to her seat,

"See, Jerry, I told you, you never believe me. Oh Jeezus, I can't stand this heat. I wish this heap would just get going. These seats are so hard, I bet the springs aren't worth shit. My back is killing me. God, I hope there's some good grass, at least, at this beach place. I'm dying to get stoned and go skinny dipping in the ocean. Fuuuuck, man, will you look at this, he's letting **MORE** people on this bus. Why don't they just wait for the next one? I just hope we get there before dark. Hey, kids, did you remember to take a leak before getting on the bus? Here have this banana, Jenny, it'll keep you from feeling like you have to barf."

The man seated next to me had opened his newspaper, trying to keep his elbows from touching mine. I urgently wanted to tell him that not all *gringos* are so coarse and impolite. We are not all the same just because we come from the same country. But I just sat there with my eyes and mouth closed, trying to pretend I didn't understand what Sal was saying, hoping I looked Italian or Spanish, anything but American.

The driver turned on the ignition of the orange and white 1963 Blue Bird, named *La Reina de la Bajura* (Queen of the Lowland). *La Reina* spewed voluminous puffs of black diesel smoke from her tailpipe. He pulled the horn chain again and slowly tried to maneuver the hulking, swaying busload onto the street leading out of town. But a small pick-up truck was parked in the way, its driver nowhere in sight. The bus driver put *La Reina* in reverse and tried again to turn the wheel enough to make the tight turn. He hooted that horn again and again, and some men chatting and smoking cigarettes in the street yelled for the owner. The door was locked, so they couldn't simply release the brake and put it in neutral to roll it out of the way. Minutes passed, and soon another bus was ready to leave, but now we were blocking its way. Finally, when no owner appeared, four young men hopped off our bus, and along with three in the street, they simply lifted the pick-up truck and carried it a short distance away from the turning radius of the bus. The *gringa* family members kept complaining loudly about the delay but entirely missed the drama in the street with the guys lifting the pick-up. (Is that where pick-up got its name?) Finally, we were moving.

The red satiny fringe that extended across the driver's windshield danced wildly, and the sequinned image of the Blessed Mother on the dashboard shimmered as the bus lurched and lumbered forward. The driver and many of the passengers crossed themselves as a precautionary measure. At only ten miles an hour, he was already shifting into the third of nine gears. The vibration in the floor tickled my feet. The man next to me seemed to recognize me from the morning, too. He asked what is almost a standard question to foreigners,

"A donde va usted? a la playa tambien?" (Where are you going, to the beach too?)

Oh, God, he's already lumped me in with these people. It's like wearing the yellow star on my arm. Why couldn't I *look* like I fit in?

"No," I told him. "I am staying with friends in Tempira and just came to Liberia to see some other members of their family, but wouldn't you know, as luck would have it, what with the festivities and all, I didn't find my friend at home. But at least I got to see her mother who is still in *luto* (mourning) after her son's death."

"Oh, where are you from?"

Good, I thought, I've confused him by the way I speak. I knew that I spoke without a detectable accent and was often complimented on that ability. I enjoyed being able to "pass" verbally.

"You're not North American, are you?" he asked, seeming almost interested in chatting.

Should I ignore the question and just keep engaging him in conversation? Or should I lie? Hesitating, I decided to answer honestly, "Yes, sir, I am."

He nodded, and raising his eyebrows and curling his upper lip, he puffed outward a short "hrumph," and turned back to his newspaper. I concluded by his reaction that he believed that *"todos somos iguales"* regardless.

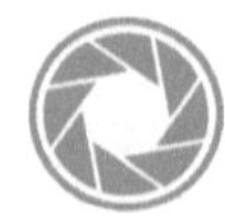

Take 2

Armando's Visit

It really was a dark and stormy night, though, after twenty-four hours, it was no longer a downpour, just a tapering-off, light rain. Even so, droplets continued to leak through the corrugated zinc roof of the old wood-frame house I was borrowing from my friend Ana. Now that Ana's father lived in San Jose in her home, and her mother had passed away, the house was unoccupied most of the year except for her brief visits and my occasional stays. The next-door neighbor, Rocio, stopped by every day to open the heavy shutters and sweep out. She had helped me find enough drinking glasses and a large pot to try to catch the plopping droplets.

There I sat, all alone, on the maroon and orange paisley crushed velvet sofa, looking at the vase of dust-laden faded plastic flowers, listening to the soothing sound of the rain on the metal roof. I closed my eyes as I reflected on my arrival and seeing people I had known for nearly twenty-five years. I took a couple of deep breaths and could feel the tension dissolve in my shoulders and gut. I was back in Guanacaste for a vacation, the first since finishing graduate school in 1986. The nighttime crowd of bugs buzzed persistently as they bumped into the bare light bulb hanging outside the front door. When I opened my eyes, I saw a thumb-nail sized frog, his tiny, suction-cupped webbed feet clinging to the turquoise-blue window jamb next to the sofa. His body was almost transparent; I could see the Lilliputian blood vessels under his smooth, rubbery, beige skin. His beady eyes bulged from the sides of his face, the little lids blinking from the bottom upwards.

It was only 8:30, too early to sleep although it was hard to keep my eyes open in the dim light, too dim to read by, but everything I'd brought to read seemed vaguely irrelevant anyway. There was no television or phonograph, and I didn't even feel like going into the bedroom to get my Walkman radio and try to tune something in. I didn't really want to listen to all that static-spattered salsa music and certainly not the soccer match with its monotonous announcer shouting "Gooooooooooool" every now and then. I'd already closed the bedroom shutter windows and door and set a burning green mosquito coil alongside the bed, so its acrid, toxic smoke would discourage those persistent beasts from staying around for an all night feast on my blood. So I sat, my attention fixed on the frog and the rain drops as they fell into the glasses I had strategically set up, feeling rather pleased with my ability to have the droplets fall dead center into the glasses. I had made minor adjustments but now very few drops were now landing on the polished plank flooring. I felt at peace.

I thought I heard a soft rap on the front door and tried not to feel afraid. Who would be coming unannounced at this hour? I had locked up for the night after Rocio left an hour or so before and hadn't heard a horse or vehicle approach or even noticed any footsteps. But the falling rain must have masked the sound. Again, a soft rap.

"Who's there?"

A low voice responded, but I couldn't quite make it out. I had a nervous suspicion who it might be.

"Who?"

"Mando," he repeated.

My heart began beating noticeably faster. What do I do? What if he's been drinking? He's strong and can easily push his way in if I even slightly open the large door, remembering another time when he had put the front paw of his black horse, Midnight, inside the house where I lived fifteen years earlier. I can't afford to create an *escándalo* in my friend's house.

I had run into Fini Fulano the day before and asked her how Mando was. Admittedly, I was curious about him after all these years. If he was *sano y bueno* (sober), I told her, it was all right to let him know I was in town, but I made her promise she wouldn't say anything to him about me until the end of my stay, and nothing at all if he was drinking. I knew he used to have a lot of land near the beach and thought it might be possible to talk to him about buying an acre or two for the future. But I had told Fini firmly to hold off telling him because I was afraid he would start coming around at all hours, especially knowing I was alone in this huge house. And if he was sober, would he soon find reasons to start drinking as a result of seeing me? Now I was irritated that Fini had broken her promise and told him so soon after my arrival. But I figured that he must be in OK condition if she had.

"Armando, *Dios mio*," I said while removing the two-by-four leaning against the door. I struggled to slide open first the lock then the floor latch on the eight-foot tall doors but finally slid open the moisture-swollen door a few inches. He grinned at me and said he'd heard from Fini that I was here and interested in buying a lot near the beach.

"Yes," I told him, "now that I have a steady job and have been saving a little money, it'd be nice to think about having a place to call my own when I visit Costa Rica, or even to think about living here again at some future time."

I had been holding my foot against the slightly ajar door. I was hoping to keep the bugs that swarmed and crashed around the outside light wouldn't also be attracted by the light inside. I felt strange talking to him without inviting him in. I knew, however, that the attentive neighbors, like Nelson the local news source, were like sentries stationed behind lacy curtains and peering between the boards nailed around their kitchen sinks. But maybe the heavy rains had distracted these small-town paparazzi, and they were too busy tending to their own leaky ceilings. After another minute or so, as I watched the bugs discovering the cracked open door, I decided to stop worrying about the grapevine *vinas* (gossips). The choice was let him in or for me to out and stand in the rain with him.

At once I felt jittery, scared, anxious, but also surprisingly pleased to see him. I didn't know quite what to say.

"*Que bueno, que sorpresa verte.* (How nice, what a surprise to see you) What a stupid thing to say. Why should I be surprised to see him?

I couldn't detect any alcohol on his breath and he looked alert and pleasant.

"Well, come in, you're getting soaked out there."

"Se puede? (May I?) *"Con permiso."* he said with the timid masculine politeness some would call the mark of a *caballero.* The intensity in his eyes, however, always had a way of throwing me off balance, negating any

of the professional persona I am usually able to maintain with the rest of the world.

I hadn't talked to him in almost fifteen years and was shocked to see that his hair was nearly all gray even though he was only forty-nine. He'd gained a lot of weight and his face was puffy, especially around his eyes. Drinking has taken a heavy toll, but still my heart was bursting with tender feelings for this man who had so intrigued and fascinated me when I first went to Guanacaste as a Peace Corps volunteer twenty-three years earlier. The high cheekbones and squinty eyes on his broad face were traits shared by everyone in his family, but his were even more marked so that some people affectionately called him *"Chino."* He looked happy to see me as he stepped into the house brushing the raindrops from his dark suntanned arms. There he stood, my archetype of the Guanacaste cowboy in his dusty suede cowboy boots, faded, tight jeans, and the crisply-pressed short-sleeved shirt still unbuttoned most of the way down showing his broad, bronzed chest with just the right amount of hair, now mostly gray, too.

More robust than he had appeared years earlier when he tried to *conquistar* me, he had not lost any of his attractiveness, even though I knew, rationally, that acting on this attraction was not a healthy instinct much less a good idea. Twenty-three years ago his insistence had always been met with my virginal rebuffs which would send him off to the *cantina* to toast his sadness and the *gringuita* he'd elevated to an unattainable icon status. It was also an excuse for drinking. He would order glass after glass of the clear fiery *guaro* chasing it with water and spitting the last swallow onto the dirt-stained floor. The scene, like a stage set, was complete with a plaintive Mexican *ranchera* sobbing from the jukebox.

"Fini told me you were here. How come you didn't let me know until now? I would have come sooner."

Just what I had thought! I couldn't tell him the truth, that I was afraid to start something I had no intention of seeing through, that he would inflate my interest to out-of-the-ball-park proportions and that was afraid I would provoke an alcoholic binge. So I just said, *"No sé"* (I don't know) and shrugged my shoulders.

He told me he'd been sitting outside the house on the cement stoop waiting for Rocio to leave. He had been watching me all that time through the cracks between the wood-plank walls of the house and remarked several times about the light reflecting off my wristwatch as I set up the glasses to catch the rain drops. He had been impatient with, even jealous, he said, of the previous visitor, feeling as though Rocío were going to stay there forever, engaging in chit-chat on time he felt should have been devoted to him. His presumptuousness and possessiveness certainly are still in tact, I thought to myself.

We had lots of catching up to do. He asked if it were true that my marriage had broken up. He told me about his kids. His oldest girl had been widowed last year when her husband of only two years was killed in an auto accident. Only one of his three boys had decided to study at the university. His two oldest boys are taller than he is. He has another son in Massachusetts whom he's never met since the mother left for the United States years ago when the child was small. He told me that he and his wife hardly talk to each other, and slipped in that he's never forgotten about me. His father died several years ago, leaving Mando alone and without a routine. He used to drive Don Daniel all around in the family Land Rover jeep, to the bank, out to inspect their *finca* near the beach, or wherever his father wanted to go. When Don Daniel died, Mando's brothers and sisters sold the car instead of giving it to him. He felt that was very unfair, but they sold it anticipating that he'd only ruin the car anyway and then it would be worthless. They treated him with considerable disdain because of his severe alcoholism, yet seemed constantly to be trying to help by checking him into a rehab center near San Jose. Once or twice they succeeded, he told me, but he "escaped" and went right back to drinking.

Mando was now the oldest surviving son since his brother Danielillo had died of a brain tumor eleven years earlier. And he was the only one of all the twelve children who, as an adult, had been the closest to his parents, partly perhaps because they continued to allow him to be a child. His own house was next door to his parents'. He always ate all his meals there. One sister told me that he had never eaten a meal prepared by his wife, even though she cooked for herself and their children. When Don Daniel died, though, his sisters had decided it would be best for their ailing mother to be moved to San Jose. That way they could each take turns caring for Doña Artemisia, and she would be near better doctors. They felt that she could no longer live alone in that big house. So now she spent two months with each of her three daughters in San Jose, with no real home of her own anymore. Occasionally they would bring her to Guanacaste to visit her other daughters, who were all quite happy not to be the ones having to care for her full time. And her *pobrecito* Mando, whom she had fervently prayed for, cried over, gone to *brujos* (witchdoctors) to seek cures for, and generally wrung her anguished hands and heart over for forty years, is now, in effect, orphaned and feeling *abandonado.*

As he talked, he moved the chair closer to the sofa and soon was sitting beside me. After a while he took both my hands in his. Those large, calloused hands that wrestled young bulls to the ground when their turn came to be castrated, that lashed hard leather *albardas* onto a horse's back in minutes, that rubbed *carbolina* into vampire bat bites on cows' necks, slathered *alquitran* around horses' ankles to protect them from tarantula bites, and lassoed runaway colts on the open *sabana* (savannah), those rough hands softly caressed mine as though he were holding a wounded sparrow. Those same hands could grip a wrist hard enough that a small woman would have a hard time pulling away should his mood become slightly more aggressive, but for some reason I never really feared that he would harm me.

We reminisced about incidents from years before: the time he'd had a few impolite words with the Peace Corps assistant director doing a "site visit" and how after that he called her my sergeant; the kiss he'd given me during a family picnic at the beach; the song *"Cerca del Mar"* that he used to play over and over again on the *rocola* as he drank alone; his huge motorcycle that could blast the whole town out of its pastoral silence.

He chuckled as he remembered all that adolescent boy behavior. I wondered to myself how far he'd really grown since those times, tying them more to the combustible fuel of alcohol than the impulses of youth. I reminded him of the gold medallion of the Madonna he had given me that I kept in a velvet box among my treasures, and the cow horn which hung with other Guanacaste *adornos* in my living room in Los Angeles. I asked if he still had the silver chain and Jewish *mezuzah* I'd given him. He said it was gone, probably lost during one of his *borracheras*, and then he asked me to give him the small gold *hamsa* amulet I now wear. When I refused, he asked me to send him a fancy western-style belt buckle from the United States.

Interspersed throughout the conversation were suggestions of intimacy that my head knew should best be avoided. He tried to flick away each of my rational explanations like used matches. I was beginning to run out of excuses, feeling like I used to feel when he pursued me. I was still afraid of insulting or rejecting him. This is not a man who takes "no" any more easily than a four-year-old boy wanting a piece of candy.

Finally, he seemed ready to give up asking and stood up to leave. I was actually pleased that he was being so mature. As we said good-night we hugged each other in a completely natural and tender embrace. Tears came to us both, and he stroked my hair as we hugged. The raindrops plopping into the half-filled water glasses and the bugs bumping into the light bulb were the only sounds about us.

He seemed contented and calm as I locked the door behind him. I washed and got ready for bed, congratulating myself for handling the potentially explosive situation so adroitly. I had managed to allow him to save face: two old friends had met and talked and acknowledged mutually good feelings, and that was it. Reflecting on the visit, I felt rather virtuous that I hadn't caused a scandal or angered Mando, and I was also pleased that I could defend myself against any innuendos from neighbors the following day. I fell asleep to the strains of some Mexican *ranchera* music from the *cantina* up the street.

Several hours later, I was awakened by the strange sound of a guitar with only two, completely out-of-tune, loose strings, being strummed monotonously and the sad voice of a drunk howling what to him was a song. He stopped every now and then to plead with me to open the window, at least to give him a glass of water to quench his thirst. There he stood, transformed in only a few hours, disheveled, incoherent, soaked to the quick, and drunkenly saying this was all my fault, that I'd left him no option because I had rejected him. I knew that no matter what, he still would have gone off and begun drinking, too, because this is a man who drinks out of joy as much as he drinks out of sorrow. I gave him the glass of water and my large beach towel to put around his shoulders and closed the shuttered window, prying his clutching fingers one by one off the sill. I felt sad but also I blamed myself, not for his drinking, but for having been curious about him in the first place. I should have known better.

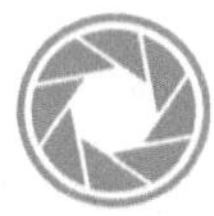

The Camera is Still Rolling

An On-Going Story

*** Excerpted from "Recuerdos de un sabanero," the personal notebook of Don Rigoberto Vargas Vargas.**

La anciedad es amarga soledad, yo vivo con dos hijos... que no me han abandonado más la madre de estos ... y dos nietecitas cariñosas .... Ultimamente nacieron tres varones que para nosotros son un encanto. . .. Pero siento soledad, de otros seres queridos, de aquellas horas felices, de mis viejos amigos, de mi mundo que se fue, dejándome una soledad terrible.

Ahora yo me pregunto ¿porqué no aprecié las cosas a su debido tiempo? ¿Porqué no fui mejor con aquellas fieles amistades que lo demostraron con hechos?

No fui mal amigo, pero mi juventud carente de comprensión, pasé inarvertidos otros deberes para con ellos, más tarde comprenderlo, me ha quedado mucho pesar por no haberos cumplido. *

My Translation

Old age is bitter loneliness. I live with two children... who have not abandoned me, plus their mother. . . and two affectionate little granddaughters. Three little boys have been born recently, which for us is charming. Even so I feel alone, away from other loved ones, from those happy hours, from my old friends, from my world that was and is now gone, leaving me a terrible loneliness.

Now I ask myself: why didn't I appreciate things at the right time? Why wasn't I better to those faithful friends who demonstrated their loyality with their deeds? I wasn't a bad friend, but in my youth, I lacked understanding. I often inadvertently overlooked other duties towards them. Having understood this too late, I am left with so much sadness for not having honored them more.

1991

Each time I say good-by, I think "This is probably the last time I shall see Don Eduardo." And each time I return for what are now merely vacations in Costa Rica, he is there, usually curled in his bed, frail, but with a surprisingly loud voice and an almost impish stare from eyes the color of a backyard swimming pool.

"Papa, look, it's Susana, " says my friend.

"Who?" he bellows.

"Susana, Susana."

"Who?"

"Su-sa-na, Susana."loudly in his ear. He no longer wears his hearing aid. Without missing a beat or giving much concern to my presence he asks, " Anita, have I eaten lunch yet?" She laughs, shrugging in my direction, and says, "*Si, papa*, you've already eaten lunch, no more until later."

"*Ya almorzé yo*?" he repeats several more times.

"*Siiiiii, papaaaa, o mi cosita linda, no recuerdes, mi preciosura, vamos papa. Le traigo un tesito, mi papasito lindo, mi bebe*," she clucks warmly in loving almost baby talk as she lightly fluffs up his pillow and adjusts the curtain next to his bed to let in the mid-afternoon light. This man used to tell me fascinating stories of his youth and write nostalgic refrains about Guanacaste. He remembered when it was only woods and tall grasslands, before it got chopped and plowed for rice, cotton and cane fields, before there was a road to Liberia and the only way to San Jose was by ferry across to Puntarenas. This man now remained oblivious to the only thin slice of wilderness visible to him through the opening in the heavy curtains: an empty lot overgrown with six-foot-tall reedy weeds.

I remain standing in the doorway, shy about approaching the old man who no longer recognizes me. I feel embarrassed and saddened by what the infirmity old age has wrought on Don Eduardo's once proud demeanor. Of all the Fulano brothers of his generation, he alone used to wear long-sleeved white shirts, buttoned tightly at the collar, even in 100° weather. Now he rests in his pajamas, an enameled chamber pot on the floor at the side of his bed.

His daughter Ana, my friend of over many decades, pampers him with the soothing voice she once used on her son, Milton, fourteen years ago as she diapered or bathed him. In part I am in awe of her ability to care for her father with such naturalness and good humor. More than once he would call her at two in the morning to go to the bathroom. Sometimes she had been so exhausted that she didn't hear the tingling bell he rang to get her attention before he had an accident. I have never known anyone to show such loving care for a parent. Sick elders are put in a "home" or have a full-time nurse to take care of the smelly tasks so everyone else is free merely to visit for a few hours, tsking and moaning about how "out-of-it" she is (hodle-bodle, as my mother used to say). There can be no expectations at all that he understands very much; but Ana, chatters lovingly to him believing he knows exactly what she is saying, and then sometimes he'll surprise her and react as if he did.

"Gabriela," she calls to the new fifteen-year-old girl she brought from Guanacaste a week earlier to help her around the house.

"*Señora*?"

"Gabriela, did papa take his walk today?" referring to the laps he would walk back and forth in the living room.

"*Si, señora*, he did a count of 300, but counting his way, you should have seen, one, two, four, seven, ten, five, fifteen, sixteen, eighteen." she said in a mildly mocking way. "But we walked until he got to 300."

"*O, mi papa* can't count right anymore, and you held on to his belt to steady him?"

"*Si, señora*" she said, nervously adjusting the large faux pearl hair barrette holding her long hair out of her no longer youthful face.

Ana senses my awkwardness and turns her attention away from her father and Gabriela. She sighs the sigh of one being pulled in many directions. Even so, she seems glad to see me and says she looks forward to spending some time with me. But she won't be able to leave her father to go to Guanacaste with me, even for a few days, especially since the *muchacha* doesn't really know the ropes yet and isn't used to the constant up and down during the night to care for Don Eduardo. Lately he's gotten night and day reversed, she tells me, sleeping away most of the day and calling her for food, trips to the bathroom, or just company during the night. Ana barely stops to take a breath as she runs her thoughts and tasks together.

She looks tired but not dejected. She gives herself little permission to resent burdens. She adores her father.

Since her mother died a few years ago, Ana is the only one to take of her father. Her son, Milton, helps a little, really an admirable amount for a young boy in my estimation, but he's a kid who has homework and needs to play. Ana's husband is a doctor who works in the hospital in another city and only comes home once or twice a week. Her brother Eddy and his wife, Haydee, and their four children are full excuses and only occasionally breeze by to say hello and spit critical comments about the care Don Eduardo is receiving.

"Why don't you ask Eddy to chip in, at least, to pay for some of the medicines or to get a night nurse to help you out?" I ask.

"Agh, Susana, *vos sabés como son ellos,* (you know how they are). Eddy just says it's impossible and Haydee couldn't care less. She'd say I'm hoarding papa's money for my own comforts. Their girls are too caught up in their social lives, and their boys are just plain lazy. They won't even help at home. That's how they've been brought up, to be *egoistas* (selfish) and *gente sin misericordia* (people without compassion). And besides, Eddy just says this is my responsibility."

"But, why?" I insist, "He's <u>his</u> father, too, and for all the schemes he pulled in the past against you, you'd think. ..." I stop and she jumps in,

" Haydee and Eddy are only out for themselves and she makes sure that whatever Eddy got from mama and papa, whether it was money, land, houses, whatever, was safely put in her own family's name and accounts. It's truly something to see. Do you remember that pasture across from the big tree on the highway? Now that belongs to her father; and the other house in front of ours? Her sister and the husband now live there. And all the acreage at San Pascual that Papa gave to Eddy she got him to sign over to her father. Don't you remember Alejandro when he was nothing, a barefoot ox-cart driver with his own father, making a few *colones* a day bringing cartloads of sand from the river? Then when he realized he could get something from mama, *vulgarmente*, he traded his fourteen-year-old daughter for the *pulperia* and all the rest kept accumulating. It was a good business deal for him to get his prettiest daughter married to my brother."

Don Eduardo is sitting up in a rocking chair as he watches television with the *muchacha* and his grandson by his side. Ana and I are sitting in the living room, eating some rice pudding she'd fixed in the morning. The late afternoon sun doesn't reach this part of the house, and I lean over to pick up my sweater from a nearby chair and to flick on the lamp sitting near my end of the sofa. It's starting to feel like old times as she tells me the latest outrages of her brother and his family. Much of our friendship is built on hours of talk and shared laments about each others' families and personal crises. Our stories are ongoing, having begun many years ago, with no way for us to mark the middle, and ending, which will only come when one of us dies, I suppose.

October, 1992: I received a birthday card from Ana with a short letter folded inside. She reported that Don Eduardo had passed away three weeks earlier. I called her the next morning. She told me that the only person who helped her during the last weeks of his life was her cousin Nuria. Neither Eddy nor their half sister Margarita had bothered to come by. Ana related how she and Nuria sat in shifts at the San Juan de Dios hospital for nearly a month. Nursing is not provided by the hospital, so family members stay with patients twenty-four hours a day. She and Nuria took turns fluffing his pillow, turning him so he wouldn't get bedsores, helping him sip cool water and take his medicines, mopping his pallid face, and talking him through the last days of his life. Given some of the past spats between the two cousins who once had been best friends, I was surprised with the news that Nuria had left Guanacaste to go to San Jose to spend so much time helping. But Don Eduardo had been Nuria's favorite uncle.

Nuria and Ana used to be very close, then about twelve years ago, something irreparable happened. A nasty bit of gossip, an ill-spoken criticism, unaccepted apologies, resulting in a coolness that permitted only superficial cordiality and civility. Trust and good humor had died. Over the years I often found myself trying to bring the two cousins, both my good friends, back together. Both resisted. As a result of their vigil during Don Eduardo's death agony. Ana mentioned Nuria's help as though it were the most normal thing. The way she said, "Nuria was the ONLY one there to help me" hinted to me that one person's dying was ushering in two others' healing.

We both hung up the phone sniffling, sighing, and looking forward to our next visit.

Mis años – by Don Rigoberto Vargas Vargas

Con escala comparo yo mis años
Y en ella me encuentro bien arriba.
Escalando mis últimos peldaños,
Y que me queda? No más que desengaños,
En el ocaso de mi pobre vida.

I compare my years to a ladder and I'm well up there,
Climbing my last rungs. And what remains?
Nothing more than disappointments
at the twilight of my poor life.

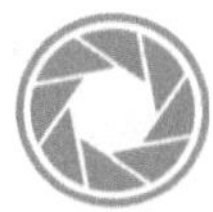

Adjusting for Clarity

A Selfie

Over the years, I have pondered and tried to understand the deeper reasons I had for joining the Peace Corps aside from those which I'd always given. Yes, I was thoroughly taken with the speech of the returned volunteer who spoke on our college campus and enthusiastically thought that I would like to try make a small contribution in a faraway land. Yes, I was inspired by John Kennedy's words ". . . Ask what you can do for your country." Yes, I thought it would be fun and adventuresome to learn about another place and people, especially after visiting the Malaysian pavilion at the New York World's Fair. But those are only partial and "official" automatic, explanations. They don't fully take into account who I was back then. They are worthy but superficial "public answers;" however, they ignore the psyche of a young girl seeking something she couldn't even articulate. To turn a phrase, I think I was Susan, desperately seeking. But what was I seeking? After all, I had every material comfort any sheltered child of the 1950s suburbs could possibly want.

When I called the Peace Corps that day in late August, eager for some word about beginning a training program in September, and they offered me the three choices of Jamaica, Honduras, or Costa Rica. I had to set aside any desire to hold out for Malaysia or another "exotic" place. I just wanted to go, and soon. They suggested I take one of the two Spanish-speaking countries since I had scored well on the language aptitude test, and they thought I'd be able to learn Spanish quickly.

Six months later, after training throughout the fall at Saint Louis University and one month of "Outward Bound" in Puerto Rico, I found myself in one of the most rural, out-of-the-way spots in Costa Rica, lacking every amenity I'd ever known. Yet for the first time in my life was actually feeling emotionally light. I wanted to live up to the Peace Corps brochure image (still concerned with images!), and was reluctant to admit to any of the hardships of living in a place such as Canalete, located about ten miles from the Nicaraguan border. The Peace Corps had gone overboard to give us tropical disease training way beyond what any of us needed to know about amoebiasis, elephantiasis, schistosomiasis, round worms, tape worms, flat worms, hookworms, and kissing bugs that seek the moisture of human lips to deposit their eggs that hatch and burrow. We also learned about malaria, tuberculosis, and other infectious diseases. We were given an experimental anti-rabies vaccine series and saw training films about these and other horrors, many of which, it turns out are not even found in Latin America. So well trained were we in the threatening water-borne or soil-dwelling tropical organisms, it was impossible to feel safe without secretly dreading contact with one or another of these *bichos.*

Every six weeks or so a rural mobile unit doctor was supposed to arrive in Canalete to give purgatives to the schoolchildren, who, an hour after taking the giant pills, would be doubled over with stomach cramps as their intestinal parasites were dislodging from their comfortable hosts. School was dismissed for the rest of the day so the children could be close to an outhouse. If the mobile doctor did not come on the scheduled day, mothers who had carried their sick children for miles in their arms would meekly turn around and walk back home, often through the rain and deep mud. They were generally resigned to such disappointments and accepted them with the same passivity as people accepted the lack of an all-weather road, well water, and fair prices.

It was the children, unabashedly curious about this newcomer, who prevented me from becoming lonely, and for that matter, ever having a moment alone, except to sleep. Many of the slides I took were of children playing, making things, climbing trees, working, or just posing in groups for my camera. An explanatory note I sent home with these slides includes one saying, "One night I was really in a poor mood and these two little girls went out and got these flowers and strung them over the little entrance way to the house to surprise me. . . ."

For the first two months I shared a little wood-frame house with another volunteer. I was the replacement she had convinced the Peace Corps was essential now that she was completing her term. She had been transferred to Canalete from a site in the south as a "punishment" for having helped another volunteer elope with an Italian count. She and I could not have been more unalike. She spoke Spanish fluently; I was just beginning. She was petite, cute, and flirtatious; I was serious, shy, and wore glasses. Because the men had sought her company, they were likewise friendly to me. The women were withdrawn and critical of her for her coquetry and likewise looked me over skeptically. Having grown up considering what other people said and thought, I found it easy to adapt to the Costa Rican version of "*Dice la gente*," ("they say") and felt that my success or failure, acceptance or rejection would be determined early by what people thought and said.

Unfortunately, we were both named Susan, were from the same country, and were members of the same organization that had descended uninvited upon this town, seemingly from nowhere. She was Susana and I was *la otra Susana* (the other Susan). It was difficult to get people to think of us as different given those three common identities, but my behavior tended to disappoint everyone. I was too shy and inhibited to flirt with the men and had no credibility with the women because I was a single woman and perhaps more, because I had no children. The "original" Susan also had no credibility with the women but she was enough of a hit with the men that she appeared to have a constituency! Being just a beginner in Spanish, I was still afraid of making mistakes and being a laughing stock. Some of the men used to ask me why I wasn't as much fun as she was.

One day during my second month in Canalete, as I was opening a can of tuna fish for lunch, I saw a small grey bird fly into the barbed-wire fence that separated the schoolyard from our little house. The children who were inside with me scurried out and ran to their father who happened to be nearby chopping some wood. He went over and picked up the bird ever so gently and began stroking it and explaining to his children that the panting bird had lost its eye and would probably never be able to fly again. Even its chances of living, he told them, were very slim. They all stood around the crouching man with curiosity and concern. I watched them from a few yards away, but my thoughts were whirling back thousands of miles and many years to the day when a sick bird had come near our house and I had picked it up and put it in a shoe box I'd lined with toilet paper. When my father found out about the bird inside the house, in my room, he became very fearful and spoke nervously about getting it outside, something about birds inside the house bringing bad luck, that it was dirty and maybe diseased. That day in Canalete gave me the first inkling that the quality of life I was going to experience in Costa Rica was different from anything I'd ever known at home. I even began to feel that I might not have so much to offer as a Peace Corps volunteer after all, and to realize that I was going to be changed in ways yet unknown.

I began to notice young boys caring for their younger brothers and sisters without the slightest embarrassment and without anyone calling them sissies. (Who back home had ever heard of a twelve or fifteen-year-old boy babysitting?). I saw fathers lovingly holding their children, explaining things to them, spending time with them. Fathers and sons, or brothers, worked together fixing fences and rain barrels, threshing rice, lugging water from the river, re-screening windows or doors, and many other things necessary for daily survival. None of the kids ever balked grudgingly, pretended that they were too busy, or acted annoyed as I used to behave when my father would ask me to run a so simple errand like going to the basement to bring him the lighter fluid to start the barbecue. I don't ever remember seeing these children shooting imaginary or toy guns at each other. Instead, they used to make playthings by rigging together all kinds of household scraps, using corn silk to make fake beards and cutting pictures from old magazines or newspapers to paste on their homemade schoolbook covers. What really struck me as remarkable was seeing sisters and brothers playing and being silly together, even teasing each other, without the battles that I had known with my sister. Yes, something did, indeed, seem different in this so-called "underdeveloped" country. True, materially they had much less than what I had been used to, but there was an abundance of something else I could feel but not articulate. Whatever it was, it had been entirely missing from my life until then.

The children became my social and work focus. They tolerated and corrected my mistakes in Spanish, often laughing mercilessly at the errors.

But their reactions felt genuine and honest, and I learned from them. We went daily to the river to bathe and would collect seeds from various plants along the banks. We strung them as beads on nylon fishing line, and I took the resulting necklaces to San Jose to be sold, dividing the money according to how many necklaces each child had made. This was their first "cooperative" entrepreneurial venture. There I was teaching them about the "joys" of business. In accord with the Peace Corps slogan, I was concerned with "helping others to help themselves"; and I can remember feeling plagued by guilt and anxiety because somehow what I was doing didn't seem as worthwhile as those volunteers working among the "needy masses" in India or Brazil that appeared on the PC advertisements. My slides and explanatory notes show efforts at pointing out visible signs of U. S. influence everywhere I looked: "Note the Alliance for Progress sticker on the big jar (of purgative pills)" and I commented frequently on what seemed like curious intrusions of the "modern, outside world" upon this "backward, underdeveloped one." I took pictures of people playing bingo, for example, and of a truck parked next to an ox cart, as though the two were anachronistic.

Early mornings in Canalete were a comfortable time once I had moved in with a family after the first Susana's departure. The smell of burning firewood in the kitchen stove blended with that of newly-dripped coffee. (The morning was filled with an orchestra of natural sounds: the calls of crows and bock-bock-bocking of hens, buzzing honey bees, clicking grasshoppers, and papery wings of swarms of dragon flies, as all these creatures went about their business of surviving. The zinc roof of the house creaked as the dewdrops condensed forming a staccato bass to the sizzling sounds of melting lard in the cast aluminum *comal* (a sort of shallow wok used in every kitchen I saw in Costa Rica). Yesterday's left-over beans and rice would get tossed together to become *gallo pinto*, Costa Rica's "typical dish," which most people, rich or poor, eat for breakfast, served up with corn tortillas and a cup of heavily sugared black coffee. The morning mist rises as the sun begins to warm the earth, and steamy dampness soon replaces any hint of cool moderation. The lower slopes of volcano Miravalles are visible, but rarely its peak, which remains covered by thick clouds. "Will the *avioneta* be able to get though the pass today?" Just in case, people hoping to leave for Cañas or Upala would walk across the rickety, swaying hanging bridge to the landing field. The dim sound of the tiny plane's single engine could be heard from miles away and, for me, at least, was a welcome and comforting sound, signifying that we were not so cut off from the rest of the world and that someone remembered this otherwise God-forsaken place. The pilot would circle and land; or he would circle and tip the wings to indicate that the runway was either too muddy or full of grazing cattle so he would not be landing that day. Disappointment.

By six o'clock in the morning, Don Rodolfo, the father in "my family," and his two older stepsons left for work, machetes and hollowed-out gourd water jugs slung over their shoulders. It was then that I learned about the many uses of a single tool. Before, I had thought of a machete as something similar to a switchblade, a lethal, hostile weapon used to intimidate or maim or worse. My New Jersey suburban world held images of young Puerto Ricans with switchblades, threatening others and themselves a la "West Side Story," so my initial reaction was one of fear when I saw a young man waving such a big, sharp knife. The machete, though, is probably the most indispensable tool of daily life in a rural, tropical area besides its work uses to *chapear*. It is useful for cutting fruit or coconuts, slicing rope, breaking up kindling sticks, and is an absolute necessity in one's constant battle with encroaching vegetation, which luxuriantly ignores man-made paths and boundaries. In just a few days' time, the weeds reassert their presence, and with it came the numerous insects which thrive in that environment and ignore all attempts to demarcate human territory. Although in the United States, people consider well-tended lawns and tastefully landscaped shrubs to be pleasing, in rural Costa Rica, a neat yard consists of well-packed dirt shaved of any hint of greenery. Domesticating the wilderness means planting in clean straight-line rows, perhaps with a few plants hanging from tin cans or enclosed in an old painted truck tire, but not anything that hints of free-flowing or random spontaneity. Keeping the area clean also helps keep snakes and other creatures from nesting close to the house.

Insects share human spaces despite attempts to keep them away. Sleeping beneath a mosquito net makes for a tranquil night's sleep, though it was habitual to inspect for mosquitoes hiding in the binding, waiting to make a feasting ground of exposed skin. (It was with some curiosity that I first observed that famous *anopheles* mosquito, which until then existed only as a word to be memorized when we studied about malaria and the building of the Panama Canal in high school. That mosquito is recognizable because it's considerably larger than ordinary mosquitoes and because of its bright irridescent blue color.)

Other precautionary measures against insects included shaking out shoes before donning them in case a scorpion had found a haven there, and checking the latrine seat for spiders or other crawling insects before sitting down on it. Summertime house flies in New Jersey were merely a nuisance, but in Canalete flies are a disgusting health menace. They buzz around the latrine hole or light in the muddy slush where the pigs lay trying to keep cool and are always ready to land on one's lunch. Mealtimes were an obsessedly two-handed activity: my right for holding the fork, the left for waving flying creatures away from the plate. But one becomes accustomed, (something that strained my mother's imagination as I'd always been a child who complained if I found even a dark speck in the milk). I certainly must have enjoyed my meals despite the inconvenience, though, having gained some ten pounds during my stay there.

Night falls early and quickly in Costa Rica, which is situated only ten or eleven degrees above the equator. In Canalete strains of *ranchera* accordion music often associated with Nicaragua (and Mexico) flow from the *pulpería* on the corner where some men might be gathered. Children run the last errands of the day for their mothers. Everyone prepares for the lights to go out whenever the *pulpería* owner shuts off his diesel-fueled generator. This can happen any time between 7:30 and 9:30 on weekdays or whenever his last customer leaves, and usually without warning. It was always a good idea to know where the nearest flashlight was for those first minutes of absolute and startling darkness. Don Rodolfo often lighted candles or his Coleman lantern if there was *canfín* (kerosene) available.

The evening meal, like the other meals, was a random affair. Everyone came to the table and ate the full plate of rice, beans, fried or boiled plantains, maybe a piece of pork, chicken, or a fried egg that Doña Juana, the mother of the family, set out. Those who drifted in later served themselves from the pots left warming on the stove. Mealtime was not the ritual gathering I had grown up with. Sometimes I would eat accompanied by one or two members of the family who did not want me to eat alone. Often the older boys would have eaten earlier and would be off somewhere chatting, reading, or listening to the radio. After I had eaten, Don Rodolfo would often bring to the table his large battery-powered radio that caught programs from San Jose, Managua, and points farther away, most memorably, Cuba. We listened to Radio Havana, fading in an out, and he would comment about the latest happenings. I truthfully do not remember what most of those conversations consisted of; but I do remember his asking me to explain all sorts of events or ideas that he just assumed I should have learned in school, things about Roman times or some other historical period. I struggled to make myself understood in my halting Spanish, frequently looking things up in my little dictionary, and he patiently corrected me or supplied a word as he listened to my explanations. Speaking about abstractions, concepts, politics, and history was a different kind of linguistic challenge than just chit-chat about the here and now.

I often look back on those after-dinner conversations as the best language classes I had. But something else became apparent to me as well. I realized that for the first time in my life an adult, fatherly type, was actually taking me, and what I thought, seriously and considering what I said to be meaningful or informative. I was 22 years old and had never before felt that a grown-up had ever heard me, Susan, not Sam's daughter, not the Gordon girl, but the me that was seeking acceptance in her own right. I think Don Rodolfo liked being able to help me learn, but he also liked, I sensed, having the opportunity to discuss, albeit on my elementary level, issues and experiences outside his enclosed world. Because I had been to college, he supposed I had encyclopedic acquaintance with history, literature, and philosophical ideas, and that I could provide some of that to him. But what used to amaze me, and still does even today when I think back to that time, was his enormous breadth of interests, curiosity, and eclectic knowledge. Before this no adult had ever asked me real questions; they were always giving me their answers. Don Rodolfo hungered for information and asked me to bring him books on one topic or another whenever I went to San Jose. I felt like a teacher, but really knew that I was the one being taught. I was not only learning to speak another language, but also to comprehend a point of reference and a world of experiences to which I had never been exposed, despite years of schooling and the availability of books and all kinds of other resources.

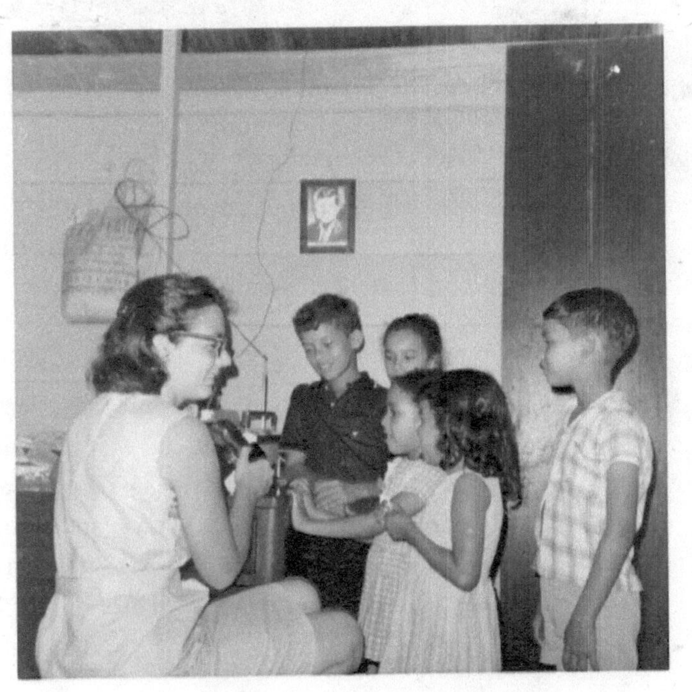

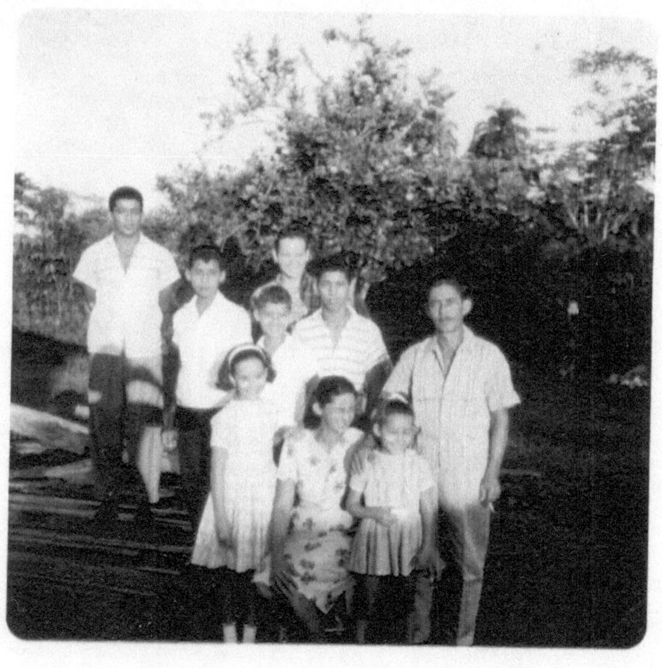

When I moved to the other side of the *cordillera* to Tempira in the province of Guanacaste, I was already fluent in Spanish, and more self-confident, not so shy or reticent. I had a different personality from Sam's daughter who arrived in Costa Rica nine months prior, a more talkative, animated, happier Susan. I found that people greeted me with the friendly and affectionate gesture of patting each other on the shoulder or upper arm that women, girls and older men do. People passing each other in the street say "*Adios,*" or stop and chat, even just to ask "*Como amaneció*? how did you wake up this morning?"

Those conversations and formative Peace Corps years gave me much that had been missing in my life: validation and approval, affection and respect. I thought it was real at the time. I found that people listened to me and didn't trivialize or infantalize me. They gave me chance to be Susana. And for those gifts I will always be grateful. And I am grateful to this day for all the experiences and ongoing friendship I cherish with Eny Maria, 60 years later and with lots still to talk and laugh about!!

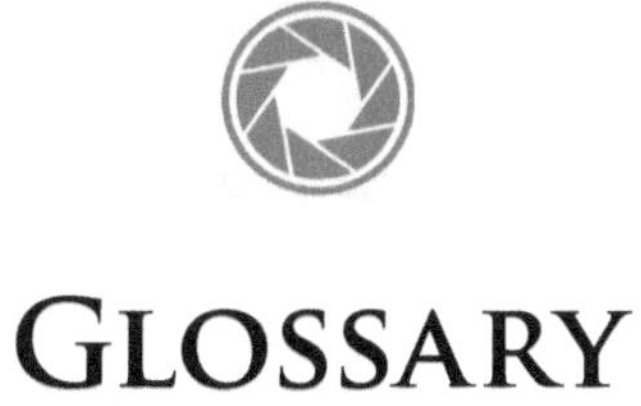

GLOSSARY

asi. como lo hago yo—Like this, the way I'm doing it

'buelita—short for Abuela, or Abuelita, Grandmother

a donde va usted? a la playa tambien—Where are you going? also to the beach?

abandonado—abandoned

accidentado—someone who is in a traffic accident

adios mi amor adios. puej—Good-bye my love (usually pronounced "goo by my lof") and once upon a time, the only phrase many boys and men knew in English.

adornos—decorations, little adornments

aires—literally, airs, but often associated with disease or catching a draft.

albarda—a Costa Rican saddle with long skirt flaps. There is no horn but instead a raised, molded portion of the leather. Usually made from cowhide and often decorated with leather tooling.

alforjas—saddle bags, typically made of woven jute, sometimes lightly decorated.
These may be slung over the horse's back, over a motorcycle seat, or merely carried on one's shoulders.

alquitrán—tar used by sabaneros to protect horses legs from spider bites

aperos—the general term for horse gear, including reins, bits, crupper, ropes, stirrups,

apíese—An order given meaning "get down off the horse"—stand on your feet

Aristides fue atropellado. Está por morirse—Aristides was hit by a car and is about to die.

así es—That's how it is, a term indicating resignation and acceptance of an unchangeable reality.

avioneta—small light aircraft used for local flights.

Ay Dios mio—Oh my God, an expression heard often

babosadas—from the literal word, droolings, but used to mean stupid actions or nonsense ramblings. A *baboso* is a stupid jerk, *babos* are drools, like what you wipe from a baby's mouth.

Baíia de Culebra—One of the lovely inlet bays along the northern coast of Guanacaste, characterized by tranquil white-sand beaches and calm, lapping water.

bajarle el piso—literally, to lower the floor from under someone. The nearest expression in English may be "Pull the rug out from under" or "cut someone down to size", but it is used with negative intentions. The idea is that if you lower the floor someone who is getting above the rest will then be no taller than everyone else because the floor beneath him has been lowered.
This action is used frequently for someone who has achieved something or excelled in ways others have come to notice and hence, resent.

la bajura—literally, lowlands (from the word bajo, low or under). This is the term that refers, often nostalgically or affectionately, to most of the area on the Nicoya Peninsula, west of Liberia. People who lived there are often called "*bajureños*"

bananera—The areas in Limon and near Golfito where the United Fruit and American Fruit companies used to have huge operations. It was the place where men from all over the country would go to seek temporary work.
The term "Banana Republic" was once used for Costa Rica because that crop dominated the economic life of the country. For accounts from the workers' perspective read *Mamita Yunai* by Carlos Luis Fallas (1941) and *Bananos y Hombres* by Carmen Lyra (1931).

barrio—neighborhood

bichos—a general term for any bugs, creatures, or intestinal parasites

bien fria—the way one orders his beer on a hot day! Really cold!

bocas (also bocadillas)—delicious small dishes of snacks served with beer or other alcoholic drinks at the cantina. These can be anything from pieces of grilled meat or chicken, tongue or liver in a tomato sauce, fish cocktail (see *ceviche)*, or when in season, turtle eggs (illegally poached from the beaches).
Sometimes cantinas are highly regarded for having great bocas. The word *boca* literally means mouth.

borrachera—a drinking session that can go on for hours or days

brillantina—once the brand name for a hair pomade but, like Kleenex, has become the eponymous term. It sometimes has a sweet-acrid smell that is not altogether pleasant. Because many people have frizzy thick hair, this pomade keeps it controllable.

brujos—literally, witches, but usually used to refer to those who dispense herbal or folk cures for anything from physical ailments to emotional distresses.

They may have magical powers like shamans or curative powers like *curanderos* but in Guanacaste, it's difficult to find out about them because most people are very discreet and fearful of being considered backward for going to these practitioners. Some of the cures may involve potions or amulets, but others can simply be folk remedies used in many parts of the word such as "cupping."

Buenos días (often pronounced in Guanacaste as Buenoh diah)—Good morning, good day

caballero—literally, horseman (caballo is horse), but has come to mean a gallant, gentleman.

cabron—literally means a male goat, but the term is used, sometimes playfully among men as a greeting ("Hey, cabron"), but also seriously to refer a man who is being cuckolded by his wife.

cajeta—a sweet, fudge-like confection made usually from sweetened milk (can be fresh, evaporated or condensed), sugar and cinnamon. Sometimes grated coconut is added as well. Homemade cajeta is much better than what is sold in the markets.

Camera de Ganaderos—Cattle ranching is (was?) the main activity in Guanacaste.
The Chamber of Cattle Ranchers is a cooperative organization centered in Liberia. There is a large building with stalls for showing cattle, and grounds with bleechers, etc. for various activities, including concerts or other civic activities.

campesina—country woman, used to define someone who lives in the rural area.

canfin—kerosene, once commonly used for Coleman lanterns, stoves, and additionally as an additive to candle wax to shine the floors. Has many household uses.

cantina—bar. Usually even very small towns boast three or four cantinas. It is a way of life for hard-working, hard-drinking men. It is usually the social center for Saturday night dances as most cantinas also have a "salon" with tables and chairs and a jukebox (rocola).

cantinera—The woman who runs the cantina. Usually a woman runs the cantina because it is attached to the house therefore a convenient way for her to earn some money AND look after the house and children. She also cooks the snacks served with drinks (see also *bocas.)*

carajo—a less than complimentary term referring to a specific "guy" (as in Ese carajo, that prick!) or as a general expression of disgust "Ay, carajo" or "Vete al carajo" (hell, or go to hell)

carbolina—carbolic acid once commonly carried by sabaneros in a carved out cow horn and used as a cure for sores on cows and horses.

carreta—Ox cart. Anyone who's been to Costa Rica knows that the painted wheel of the ox cart is the national "logo." There's a big one in the airport and miniatures of varying sizes are available at all tourist shops and in Sarchi, the town most associated with the production of the painted ox carts. In Guanacaste, the oxcarts do not enjoy the painted designs of in the central valley areas (San Jose and environs are called the Meseta Central)

Cartagos—refers in general to people who live in the Meseta Central, but specifically to the light-skinned natives of Cartago, a province just outside San Jose, and once the original capital of Costa Rica when it was a Spanish colony.
The basilica of the Virgin of Los Angeles is situated in Cartago. Guanacastecos sometimes refer to Cartagos in ways suggesting they are less astute than the locals.

causa—cause, as in a political movement or cause

cenícero—ash tree

ceviche—a delicious fish cocktail made from bits of cut up raw fish marinated for several hours in lemon juice, coriander leaves (cilantro or culantro), and other seasonings.

charro—large Mexican hat usually associated with mariachi musicians but also a popular tourist item in Mexico.

chícheme—a fermented corn drink usually made and sold during popular fiestas or other similar occasions.

chotear—to gossip

chunches—stuff, things, assorted items, junk. In the singular, may be used like "thing-ama-jig, referring to any undefined thing.

ciao—adopted from the Italian as a farewell

cobrador—the young fellows on buses who go to each person and collect the bus fare

cochino—piglike, dirty

colegio—secondary school, after 6th grade. Up to sixth grade was mandatory and paid for the by state. Post primary schooling is not free or mandatory.

Colon, colones, pl.—Costa Rican currency. Named after Christopher Columbus (Cristobal Colon). Used in other countries, as well, including El Salvador.

comal—a gently curving, wok-like cooking pan, often made of iron or ceramic.
The curved bottom was especially useful for sitting on the open hole in the old wood-burning stoves before gas ranges became popular.

comandancia—Central command police headquarters

cómo amaneció—literally, "how did you awaken?" but used familiarly as an early morning greeting instead of "Buenos dias" in many cases. In English we might say the reverse, "how did you sleep?" or "did you sleep well,"

con permiso—Excuse me, literally, with your permission. The other person might answer with "suyo" or "propio," meaning "yours."

congos—monkeys, usually refers to Howler monkeys who populate the trees near rivers.

conquista—conquest. May be used in the larger sense (with a capital C) to refer to the Spanish Conquests of Latin America in the 16th century. But also means the male achievement of winning over a lady's heart and all the rest of her, for that matter.

conyuge—team of oxen or marital partner (from the Latin conjugal)

cordillera—the range of volcanic mountains running through all of Costa Rica.
Actually these mountains begin with the Rockies in the north and continue all through Mexico, as the Sierras, through all of Central America, becoming the Andes in South America. Specifically, in Costa Rica, the Cordillera divides the country into various climates. To the east the weather is very humid and rainy much of the year; to the west, the climate is arid with seasonal winds and well-defined periods of rain and dry spells.

Corpus Cristi—literally, body of Christ, this is a Catholic religious festival marked in small towns with a procession that stops at each corner where neighbors have built elaborately decorated altars. It is celebrated the Thursday after Trinity Sunday.

Cortez—a beautiful, yellow or pink flowering tree often used along a roadside or property fence line.

coyol—a large tree that can be tapped for a sweet liquid which ferments as it ages and is served as a beverage. The drink is also called *coyol.*

creida—snooty or stuck up, literally believing too much in yourself.

Cristianos—Literally Christians, but can also be used in a context to mean human beings (of the Christian faith only), as in a town census. This may stem

from that usage by Catholic missionaries who traveled with the Spanish conquerors and converted souls along the way, noting their numbers in old records; or more currently, used to define those who have become Evangelical Christians. They are also called "Evangelicos."

cuartel—the provincial jailhouse or military headquarters

Cuerpo de Paz—Peace Corps, referring both to the organization or to the individual members.

cuidador—caretaker, watchman

culto—literally, cult, but now refers to the Evangelical meeting houses in small towns.

dama—lady, in the gallant sense like caballero is for gentleman.

deja, hombre—Leave it, man

dejen de joder—Quit bothering me, or more roughly, "Stop messing with me."

deme más, urrrrria, periquito—little sounds when talking to a parakeet. They like the sound of the rolling "r" and learn to imitate it.

dice la gente—People say, or "they" say, everyone says—the impersonal, authoritative way to pass along information, opinion, judgement, and most importantly, gossip.

Dios mio—My God!

directora—school or organization director

discomovil—a mobile disk jockey unit that is hired to supply recorded music for a dance at a cantina. Most people preferred live music but the discomovil became very popular as electricity and roads improved.

docoma—a light weight, cotton blend fabric, usually used for making school uniform blouses or other shirts that didn't require much ironing.

Don—respectful term of address used with a man's first name.

Doña—respectful term of address used with a married woman's first name

Duendes—in Costa Rican folklore, little elf-like creatures said to dress in red outfits and do mischievous things. They are sometimes accused of kidnapping children or luring them away with candies or toys. Duendes are said to leave tell-tale signs, especially backwards footprints. Some people used to tie children to the bed or table leg during the day to make sure they wouldn't be taken by the duendes.

egoistas—selfish people

El Cadejos—a character in Costa Rican folklore in the form of a black dog with chains who is said to help and accompany drunks safely back home at night.

El Consentido—The Spoiled One, the name of a local bus. Generally, all Costa Rican buses (and even some airplanes) have names. They can be after girlfriends, or be romantic slogans such as "flower of the Pampa," "Queen of the Bajura" and so on. Buses were always highly decorated, especially the back and side panels, with murals or elaborate designs. Even inside the buses, over the windshield or on the dashboard, drivers (often the owners) hung all kinds of decorative things, religious statues or pictures, baby shoes, and more.

el zarpe—from the word "zarpar" to set sail, this word is used to indicate (supposedly) the last round of drinks. There often turn out to be many zarpes. Setting sail may be an appropriate term since they often leave the cantina "three sheets to the wind."

elaborado en Guatemala—Manufactured in Guatemala.

empanadas—literally, embreaded, like turnovers made with pastry dough and filled either with meat and vegetables, or more typically in Costa Rica, with sugar and cinnamon. Best eaten warm!

es la voluntad de Dios—It's the will of God.

escándalo—a scene, a scandal

está loca—she is crazy

fiestas—festivals. Each community has annual civic festivals that draw people from all around the area. There are also religious festivals. These occasions usually take place over an entire weekend and involve lots of food, drinking, and dances at night. During the day there may be bull riding, horse processions (tope de caballos), and other horse games with prizes.

finca—farm

fotonovela—magazines that have photographed panels and dialogue in "balloons" like comic books

frontera norte—northern border between Costa Rica and Nicaragua

gallo pinto—literally spotted rooster, but in Costa Rica, this dish is the typical breakfast food in nearly the whole country, among all socio-economic groups. It is made by frying together leftover beans and rice until the rice is crispy and the beans are no longer wet. Often *gallo pinto* is served with *natilla*, a kind of sour cream, or with white cheese and tortilla.

garrobo—a local kind of iguana. Nicaraguans and some Costa Ricans use this as a chicken substitute but many people look down on this practice.

There's a rest stop along the Interamerican highway just before entering Guanacaste with several restaurants. *Dice la gente* that you shouldn't order chicken soup (*sopa de gallina*) there because it will be made with *gallina de palo*, a tree chicken, meaning a garrobo.

garzas—white cattle egrets. These birds have a symbiotic relationship with the cattle, often perching for hours on a cow's back and picking out the bugs and flies from its hide.

gente sin misericordia—merciless people

granizados—shaved ice in a paper cone topped with red sugar syrup and condensed milk. Men have special carts for large blocks of ice and a metal device for hand shaving and colleting the ice to pour into the cone. This was especially popular before commercial ice cream and popsicles were available in this hot climate.

gringa—a North American female*; gringo* – North American male

guacal—Before plastic jugs and strainers became available, people made sieves, bowls, cups, and water canteens from the squash-like fruit that grows on the *jícaro* tree. Many artistic men carved beautiful designs in them while still green. As they dried out, they hardened with the etched designs. For regular household use, though, they were left plain. They might be used for scooping water for cooking, bathing, etc., or for scooping up or carrying quantities of rice and beans from sacks.

Guardia Rural—local community police. While Costa Rica likes to boast about not having a military, there are various levels of policing. In the old days, the local Guardia only carried a night stick and wore yellow shirts. They did not carry a weapon. Today, I believe they are armed.

guaritos—little chocolate candies filled with sugar-cane rum (guaro). The candies are individually wrapped and can be bought singly or in bags.

guaro—the bane or delight of many, this clear, local sugar-cane rum is strong and quickly intoxicating. Every local bar is well stocked with guaro and beer

guarumo y junquillo—shrubs whose leaves have medicinal properties, considered especially good for making infusions for hot compresses to apply to arthritic or stiff joints.

güiski—Costa Rican for "whiskey"

hasta luego—See you later

hasta mañana—See you tomorrow

hasta pronto—See you soon

hecho en El Salvador—made in El Salvador

hola—Hi

humilde—humble, simple

ICE, Instituto Costarricense de Electricidad—National Electricity Company of Costa Rica

idiay—an expression used sometimes a greeting when waiting for something to be done. Roughly, used as "and so?" or "so what's going on?"

ignorancia—ignorance

indirecta—an indirect insult said behind someone's back but in her presence.

lorita—little parrot (lora is parrot)

'jueputa—short for hijo de puta, son of a whore

La Cegua—In Costa Rican folklore, this is a beautiful woman who stands by the side of road at night and appears to be asking for a ride from a passing horseman. He gladly picks her up, but when he turns around to look at her, or in some accounts, when she gets down where he takes her, her face turns into that of a skeleton. This is a character who appears in the folklore of other Latin American countries, as well. There are numerous studies—see, for instance, work by Shirley Arora from UCLA.

La Llorona—The Weeping Woman, a folk character, whose wailing can be heard at night near river banks. She apparently searches for her children whom she is said to have drowned. There are numerous versions of the story and popular throughout Mexico and Central America. There is also a well-known popular song by the same name.

luna menguante—the waning moon, getting smaller after the full moon. Many farmers plant according to the phases of the moon, considering the gravitational pull of the moon to affect the growth of the different crops. For instance, corn, sorghum, beans, and rice, should be planted when the moon is growing (*la luna creciente*) because these plants need to grow upwards.
On the other hand, root crops like yucca (manioc) need to grow strong and deep in the earth so should be planted when the moon is waning.

La Mona—Another folklore figure, also sometimes called La Mica. The belief is that this is a woman who seduces a man and then shows up at his house the next day asking for salt from his wife. She then turns into a monkey and sits in the tree near the house.

la señora de—literally, Mrs., but also used in an ironic way to indicate a woman who has taking on matronly, high-status airs now that she has married a well-to-do man.

La Virgen de Los Angeles—The patron saint of Costa Rica, said to have made a miraculous appearance to a simple peasant in Cartago in the 17th century on the site of the current basilica bearing her name.

lagartos—alligators

laka-laka—gossip, the "latest"

Las Espuelas, El Bramadero, Los Boyeros, La Ronda—hotels in Liberia named for items associated with the cattle ranching and cowboy atmosphere.

le canta la gallina—literally the hen sings to him, but means that a man is "henpecked."

Liberacion Nacional—A dominant social-democratic party that rose to prominence under the leadership of Jose (Pepe) Figueres after the 1948 civil war.

Liberacionistas—members of the *Liberacion Nacional* party

limonada—lemonade

lo siento—I'm sorry

lo típico—typical. Often refers to traditional foods, dances, and other aspects of folklore

luna creciente—see luna menguante

luna liberiana—a popular folk song celebrating the full moon in Liberia as it casts its white light on the white clay landscape

luto—period of mourning during which female family members wear black.
Widows often continue to wear black many years after the death of her husband.

macho mula—a male mule (cross between a horse and a mule). Considered very good and strong as work beasts.

mal ojo—Evil eye. There are whole books written on the subject (see work by Alan Dundes). Various measures and amulets are used to protect oneself and one's home from the evil eye.

manila—a large jute rope used by cowboys primarily to lasso animals

marañones—cashew fruit

marimberos—those musicians who play the long xylophone made of wood and sculpted gourds. Originated, apparently, in Africa, but very popular in various other countries of Central America, notably Nicaragua and Guatemala.

me hace daño—this is harmful to me; a believable way to excuse oneself from doing something he doesn't want to do.

mezuzah—Jewish ornamental case with the "Shma Israel" prayer inside it to love God and obey His commandments at all times. Jewish homes have these on the doorposts, but also some people wear small ones on chains around their neck.

miembro del Cuerpo de Paz—Peace Corps member

mire—Look!

moda—style

molestones—bothersome individuals

mondongo—a strong smelling soup made with tripe

muchacha—girl

natilla—sour cream

nécios—annoying individuals

nido de macuá—in folk belief, the nest of the macua, a small bird, is supposed to help safeguard a home. I am not familiar with the bird.

niña—little girl, but also used as a respectful form of address for an unmarried teacher or young woman from a well-to-do family.

Noble Patria, tu Hermosa bandera, expression de tu vida nos da "...bajo el limpido azul de tu cielo, blanca y pura descansa la paz."—first and last lines of the Costa Rican national anthem.

norteamericano—North American, gringo

nos vemos—be seein' you

novillos—year old uncastrated bulls

números, compre pedazos de lotería!—the cry of lottery ticket vendors

ojo caliente—hot eye, something like the Evil Eye, mal ojo

ojo de agua—spring of water

oscuro—dark

Pampa Guanacasteca—The open grassy plains, similar to the cattle raising areas of Argentina

panga—a small boat, often a dugout from a large tree such as a *cenícero* tree which grows near river banks

para no cansarle con el cuento—To make a long story short...

paseos—outings, short pleasure trips, a walk

pata caliente—literally a hot foot, a gad-about, usually a woman who doesn't like staying in the house and is seen all over town.

patrón—boss

payasadas—clowning behaviors

peones—day workers, usually working in the fields

pesetas—one quarter of one colon; coins that used to be fed into the jukebox

Pilsen—name of a local, lager beer

plaga—plague

plaza—central, open area in front of the church in traditionally laid-out towns.

pobre diablo—literally poor devil, and used in the same sense as in English to refer to a man with bad luck. (See *Memorias de un Pobre Diablo* by Hernan Elizondo Arce, 1969)

pobrecito—poor thing

polacos—refers to the traveling peddlers who used to come from San Jose and sell dry goods, especially fabrics. They sold with terms of credit. Most of these salesmen were Jewish immigrants who had come from Poland. Most Guanacastecos were not familiar with the word "judio" meaning Jew or Jewish but they, unfortunately, used the term "polaco" similarly pejoratively mainly because they were associated with collecting past due bills.

preparacion—literally, preparation, but this refers to the amount of schooling one has. Not to be confused with *educacion* (education), which really refers to behavior, being polite, minding one's manners, etc. In other words, someone can have many years of schooling (*preparacion*) and still be boorish and unmannerly, in Spanish "*mal educado*"

propio or *suyo*—Yours (see *con permiso*)

pulman—large inter-region buses with comfortable seats, luggage storage. Costa Rica has a very good system of inter-region buses.

pulpería—small general store

pura película—a show off

puta—whore

quien sabe?—Who knows?

rancheros and *boleros*—kinds of songs

raspa—leaves with a scratchy texture

recuerdo—a souvenir

regaño—scolding

remedios—folk remedies, cures. Can be leaves, potions, or practices such as cupping, or laying on of hands.

rocola—jukebox, usually the big Wurlitzer with colored lights

rosquillas—baked corn dough mixed with white cheese and shaped like small flat rings. Usually served with coffee, they are not sweet.

sabanero—Cowboy, with a similar romanticism as the Argentine *gaucho.*

sacos de plagas—Literally, bag of plagues. This is often used in reference to someone who complains and complains about real or imagined problems, to the point of seeming like a person with the worst luck in the world.

sahinos—wild pigs that used to be hunted at night for food.

salones—the open area used for dancing in the cantina. Salon may also be the living room in one's home.

sano y bueno—literally, healthy and good, but used to refer to someone who has stopped drinking and is sober. Sometimes only a temporary state.

sardinas—Little fish that swim near the edges of the river. Their nip is more annoying than harmful

se puede?—May I? A polite way to request entry into a house or to ask to be seated.

Semana Santa—Holy Week, Easter Week

Señor Ministro—Mr. Minister, the way to address the head of a government ministry.

serape—The colorful, woven, striped blanket made in Mexico and often worn over the shoulder.

serenata—Serenade, once a gallant and romantic way for a young man to show special attention to a lady he was trying to "*conquistar*"

si Dios quiere—God Willing, this expression is often a response to almost anything that one feels powerless to control or something in the realm of wishful thinking

siete frijoles—7 beans

siete perjumes—7 perfumes

sindicalistas—labor union members

tanelas—small square cakes made with corn meal, cheese, sugar, and cinnamon

telegrafista—the telegrapher

tepisquintle—a small nocturnal rodent that used to be hunted for its meat

típico—typical

todos somos iguales—a watchword characterizing Costa Ricans' view of what democracy means: We are all equal.

tope de caballos—A parade with horses dressed with special ornaments and beautiful saddles.

traguito—a small drink, as in "just one more little drink, then we'll go."

Tropigas—the name of the propane (bottled) gas used for cooking. There is no natural gas in Costa Rica.

vampiros—vampire bats that attack livestock as well as human beings.

vaquetas—a soft, usually deer skin, saddle covering. These are highly prized and quite expensive.

vinas—gossipy women. There was a radio program for many years called "Viniando con Doña Vina," featuring a woman known for passing along all the latest tidbits in a series of funny conversations.

vos sabés como son ellos—You know how they are! Costa Ricans use "vos" as the familiar form of you more than they use "tu."

vulgarmente—vulgarly

ya almorzé yo—I have already eaten lunch

yuca—a root (tuber) boiled and fried. Also known as manioc. Yuca used to be a staple crop along with beans and rice.

yugo—the yoke holding oxen together. In Guanacaste, these are not highly decorated or painted as they are in the areas around San Jose.

zopilotes—buzzards, birds that eat dead animals. Sometimes people use the term to talk about other people who hover around to take advantage of someone's bad luck or, worse, death.

www.ingramcontent.com/pod-product-compliance
Lightning Source LLC
Chambersburg PA
CBHW022052050726
47591CB00002B/499

9781963068702